THE IMMERSIVE CLASSROOM

Create Customized Learning Experiences With AR/VR

JAIME DONALLY

International Society for Technology in Education
PORTLAND, OREGON • ARLINGTON, VIRGINIA

The Immersive Classroom
Create Customized Learning Experiences with AR/VR
Jaime Donally

© 2021 International Society for Technology in Education

World rights reserved. No part of this book may be reproduced or transmitted in any form or by any means—electronic, mechanical, photocopying, recording, or by any information storage or retrieval system—without prior written permission from the publisher. Learn more at iste.org/resources/thought-leadership/permissions-and-reprints.

Director of Books and Journals: *Colin Murcray*
Acquisitions Editor: *Valerie Witte*
Managing Editor: *Emily Reed*
Editor: *Courtney Burkholder*
Proofreader: *Laura Gibson*
Indexer: *Wendy Allex*
Book Design and Production: *Jeff Puda*
Cover Design: *Beth DeWilde*

Library of Congress Control Number: 2020949337

First Edition
ISBN: 978-1-56484-853-6
Ebook version available.

Printed in the United States of America.
ISTE® is a registered trademark of the International Society for Technology in Education.

About ISTE

The International Society for Technology in Education (ISTE) is a nonprofit organization that works with the global education community to accelerate the use of technology to solve tough problems and inspire innovation. Our worldwide network believes in the potential technology holds to transform teaching and learning.

ISTE sets a bold vision for education transformation through the ISTE Standards, a framework for students, educators, administrators, coaches and computer science educators to rethink education and create innovative learning environments. ISTE hosts the annual ISTE Conference & Expo, one of the world's most influential edtech events. The organization's professional learning offerings include online courses, professional networks, year-round academies, peer-reviewed journals and other publications. ISTE is also the leading publisher of books focused on technology in education. For more information or to become an ISTE member, visit iste.org. Subscribe to ISTE's YouTube channel and connect with ISTE on Twitter, Facebook and LinkedIn.

Related ISTE Titles

Learning Transported: Augmented, Virtual and Mixed Reality for All Classrooms by Jaime Donally

Chart A New Course: A Guide to Teaching Essential Skills for Tomorrow's World by Rachelle Dene Poth

About the Author

A former PK-8 math teacher turned technology integration specialist, Jaime Donally has spent more than a decade at the classroom and district levels thinking about how educators can practically use augmented, virtual, and mixed realities. In her current role as an independent education consultant, she provides professional development on immersive technology to districts and at conferences. She also runs a weekly Twitter chat about AR and VR in education. Donally is the author of *Learning Transported*, which aims to tackle the fears and hurdles of immersive reality integration, and get teachers on board with successful implementation.

Acknowledgments

As I began the journey of writing my second book, I was given the blessing of time and encouragement from my friends and family. The effort of establishing a new consulting business, the loss of family members, and the challenges of a global pandemic all seemed to stall the possibility that this book would ever come to fruition. Writing is a genuine struggle for me, and my dependence on God was daily. I absolutely found His power through my weakness.

I could not have completed this project without my husband Frank consistently reminding me to take it one day at a time. He diligently worked on his dissertation while motiving me to keep going. It was my children—Elias, Hannah, and Elliana—who regularly evaluated augmented and virtual reality tools so I could confidently recommend the best resources. They are the classroom experts on this topic and I have no doubt that their knowledge of immersive technology will help them in their future careers. I'm incredibly grateful to my family for supporting me, through prayers and love, to finish this journey.

A special thanks to Jimmy, Jesse, Jolee, Jayden, Jace, and Chelsea Lynn for taking on every AR/VR challenge I shared while providing a weekend escape from work to gather as a family.

My sincere appreciation to Marialice, Rachelle, Andi, the Global Maker Day organizing team, and my53's, who regularly check-in and give recommendations to keep moving forward. You've been there through the joy and the pain and I deeply value our friendship.

Thanks to the #ARVRinEDU community, who shared inspiring ideas week in and week out to support classroom innovation around the globe. These educators went above and beyond to regularly support others: Linda, Katie, David, Kim, Denise, Caitlin, Drezek, Priscilla, Alfonso, and Maria.

Finally, I want to appreciate my mom for giving me the confidence to pursue my passion. The constant reminder that I can do anything has spilled over into every aspect of my life, making risk taking my normal practice. I can't imagine who I would be without you in my life, and I'm so blessed to call you my mom.

Dedication

This book is dedicated to Papi, who never asked for anything
but a bucket of $100 bills! We will all meet you one day in paradise
and forever have fun, fun, fun together.

Contents

Foreword ix
Introduction 1
    Immersive Technology..2
    How to Use This Book...3

CHAPTER 1

Benefits of Immersive Technology in Education................................6
    Student Engagement 7
    Student Investment..9
    Flexibility...10
    Student Challenge 11
    A Success Story with AR/VR from My Own Life....................................12

CHAPTER 2

How to Use Immersive Technology to Personalize Learning............15
    Identify Areas of Need 16
    What Immersive Technology Is Right for Your School? 17
    AR/VR Offers Accessibility...17
    A Success Story with AR/VR from My Own Life....................................19

Contents

CHAPTER 3

App Hacking 21
    Push the Limits of Tools to Find New Capabilities 22
    Nearpod App Hacking Example..22
    WallaMe App Hacking Example 23
    EyeJack App Hacking Example 25
    Share Ideas with Immersive Technology Companies 26

CHAPTER 4

App Smashing..28
    App Smashing in Action: Flipgrid and MERGE Explorer 29
    Smashable Video Tools 30
    App Smashing with AR Creation Tools 31
    App Smashing with VR 34
    App Smashing with Oculus Quest 36
    Virtual Meeting Spaces 38
    Combined AR and VR Examples..39

CHAPTER 5

Personalized Devices..42
    Remote Learning..43
    What to Look for in Immersive Technology Devices 44
    Cross-Platform Learning 46
    Kit Ideas..48
    Grant Possibilities 51

CHAPTER 6

AR/VR in the Classroom: Personalized Experiences 52
    Scavenger Hunts with Scavengar EDU 52
    Breakouts Using CoSpaces 54
    Science Labs 55
    Interactive Presentations with JigSpace......................................60
    Create Your Own Augmented Reality...61
    Limited by Location? 360-Degree Learning Can Help.............63

CHAPTER 7
AR/VR in the Classroom: Immersive Activities to Inspire Learning ..65
   Writing and Literacy Tools...66
   Immersive STEAM Activities..69
   Tools to Foster Problem Solving and Collaboration Skills 71
   Health and Physical Education Tools 73

CHAPTER 8
Personalized Experiences for All Students 76
   Targeted Technology 77
   One Size Does Not Fit All 83
   Student Ownership 84
   Student Voice and Choice 84
   Passion-Based Learning 86
   Student Leadership 87

CHAPTER 9
Personalizing Professional Development..89
   Personalized Learning for Educators 90
   BuildingCommunity with ARVRinEDU..92
   The Immersive Experience..97
   Immersive Technology in Social Media 99
   ISTE Standards for Educators..100
   VR Meeting Spaces 103
   #GlobalMakerDay 106
   Conclusion 107

Appendix: AR/VR Resources 108
References 125
Index..126

Foreword

Let's begin with the title of this book, which immediately invites readers to immerse themselves into a personalized learning experience with AR/VR. *The Immersive Classroom: Creating Customized Learning Experiences with AR/VR* is not just a how to get started book, but is an invaluable resource with stories that connect to all types of learning styles. No matter where you find yourself on your immersive technology journey, this book empowers you as a learner while raising awareness to ensure that immersive technologies are accessible for all.

As an untraditional learner myself, I initially thought immersive technology was just for technology enthusiasts. As I've been a part of the ARVRinEDU community for years now, I've learned that immersive technologies are for *everyone*. Jaime Donally has always put the focus on human needs before technology. Over the years, she has built an inclusive global community where meeting the needs of individual learners is her top priority. This customized approach meets the learner where they are and highlights their abilities instead of their disabilities.

I've been blessed to share the stage with Jaime as we have co-presented about digital citizenship and emerging technologies. For me, what Jaime does is different than others in this space because she focuses on a personalized approach to learning and embeds standards and skills into everyday lessons and routines, making immersive technology not just an add-on, but rather an extension to learning through powerful and personal experiences.

THE IMMERSIVE CLASSROOM

In the world of digital citizenship, we are always looking for authentic ways to help students be alert, balanced, engaged, informed, and inclusive. More importantly, we are interested in making digital citizenship a verb—something we actively do every single day. Jaime is able to champion learning through action, which she shares through powerful stories of students and classrooms immersed in learning.

As a conductor leads an orchestra, Jaime leads us in an exploration of AR/VR through the same process. Each instrument has a place and purpose in a musical composition, and the conductor brings all the unique contributions together. In the same spirit, Jaime has curated resources and tools that can be combined to create powerful immersive learning experiences. She guides us in our exploration with links to content, 3D objects, and videos throughout the entire book. Each chapter concludes with an Immersive Learning Challenge that allows us to take what we've learned and encourage our students to experience a variety of AR/VR tools and platforms.

The Immersive Classroom: Creating Customized Learning Experiences with AR/VR reminds us that immersive technologies are for all ages and all abilities. The book is a wonderful invitation for us to learn together, side-by-side, as Jaime leads us through a personalized learning experience with AR/VR.

Marialice B.F.X. Curran, Ph.D. is internationally recognized as a pioneer in digital citizenship. Dr. Curran has served as an associate professor, middle school teacher and head of middle school, and is currently the founder of the Digital Citizenship Institute and the Digital Citizenship Summit™. She co-authored DigCitKids: Lessons Learning Side-by-Side to Empower Others Around the World with her son and guides school communities around the world through her IMPACT model to use technology for good in school, home, play, and work.

Introduction

There was once a student who had never read a book from cover to cover until the last year of high school. This student found ways to bypass the required reading by listening to conversations in class or by looking at the pictures, reading a few sentences of each chapter, or reading the back cover to find the answers. The student would employ every possible strategy to avoid reading, and if the assignments were impossible without having read the book, they would never get completed.

This student experienced a lack of reading in their home environment. The reading options in school rarely took into account student preference, and there was no expectation to complete every assignment or to perform beyond passing a class. The student's decision to avoid reading stemmed from a lack of interest, and it wasn't until the last year of high school that she was presented with an opportunity to read for enjoyment. When reading time was required at the beginning of class, the student was able to focus and was presented with a choice of what to read. Soon, what started out as a daunting task became enjoyable.

How does a student go through nearly all of her school years without completely reading a book? Why was this student never offered a book that she found engaging enough to keep reading? How can a student be so disengaged in the classroom and not held accountable for the resulting lack of understanding? Would you believe that the student later became an educator? Would you believe that the student was me?

Fast forward to a decade later. After having my children, I decided to pursue an advanced degree in education in order to be the "best homeschool parent." It didn't take long to realize how much I needed a community of experts to support me as I endeavored to help my children thrive in education. In my education courses, I realized how passionate I was about supporting children to see their full potential, and to set their goals and expectations high. It became clear that I wanted to become a teacher to believe in and help those students who needed it most.

Desire to fully engage my students' interest is the main reason I feel so passionate about personalized learning with augmented reality (AR) and virtual reality (VR) and the exciting opportunities for using immersive technology (the umbrella term for AR and VR as well as mixed reality [MR]) in the classroom. When a student (like me!) is presented with material they find utterly uninteresting, and on top of that experiences no external pressure to excel, they are likely to be left behind. I have found that there is a multiplicity of ways to teach and learn with AR/VR, and although each learning experience likely will differ, they all have one thing in common: student engagement. When sharing immersive technology with educators, I often hear the comment that AR/VR experiences would have changed their learning journey, and I couldn't agree with them more.

Immersive Technology

The kind of captivating deep dive into learning led by Miss Frizzle of The Magic School Bus book series is not only possible but could be immediately available to many classrooms through immersive technology. Using AR/VR tools that are easily accessible on mobile devices, our classrooms can be filled with exciting learning adventures every day.

We hear about the many benefits of personalized learning for our students. From customized lesson plans to student ownership, we recognize that our schools should assess the individual student rather than take a one-size-fits-all approach. As we continue to adapt to the needs of each student, our instructional approach and practices must also adapt to the ever-changing field of education. AR/VR offers a powerful way to support every type of learner. Instead of approaching content or projects in a typical lecture and assignment fashion, just imagine, for example:

- walking into an augmented reality portal to see and hear the rushing water of Niagara Falls;
- collecting artifacts from the battle of Gettysburg;
- holding a beating heart in your hand using an AR object (the MERGE Cube);
- collaborating with students around the world in virtual reality; or
- engineering VR meeting spaces to fit the needs of your community.

From numerous tasks, physical and emotional demands, data, more data, and paperwork, who can offer anything more? So much of the teacher's schedule is filled with tasks that pull our attention away from our students. Most educators are struggling just to keep up.

Here's the good news: when introducing AR/VR, the goal is to eliminate additional work. I believe AR/VR has the capability of reigniting your passion for teaching and learning. Using AR/VR can engage our most reluctant students to want to understand the material and dig deeper into the content. These tools shouldn't add a burden on educators but rather should improve our lessons to make teaching and learning more enjoyable and beneficial for all.

How to Use This Book

When I wrote *Learning Transported* (2018), my goal was to build the foundation for AR/VR in education, introduce new vocabulary and resources, and address misconceptions about immersive technology in the classroom. The book was intended to inspire educators to embrace this new technology with a plan and to avoid potential obstacles along the way.

This book goes beyond the inital steps of understanding and incorporating AR/VR tools for the classroom and focuses on harnessing the tools to make them work for your individual learners. Each classroom will look different in its approach to AR/VR, because each classroom has students with varying individual learning styles. By understanding what the technology can offer, and through combining or hacking tools to customize the experience, you can personalize these experiences for every student.

Features

This book features interactive content incorporated into each of the images so that you can truly experience the different tools and see the examples played out. These images (AR triggers) link to bonus content, 3D objects, and videos that provide additional support and a way to engage further in the material. Look for the QR codes and instructions that accompany the images, and have fun exploring the tools—all of which are freely available on iOS and Android devices. For easy reference, Table 0.1 lists all of the tools required to access the interactive content.

Another way to engage with the book is through participating in challenges. At the end of every chapter, I share an Immersive Learning Challenge. These challenges are intended to help you bring AR/VR to your students and give them an opportunity to demonstrate their learning. Please share student responses as well as your own experiences using immersive technology on social media using #ARVRinEDU.

The book concludes with an appendix of over 100 AR/VR tools to help in your journey of creating customized immersive experiences. Along with how to access the tool, the appendix shares recommended grade level and content area.

> **Don't miss the front cover experience of the book** using the Halo AR app by LightUp. Open the Halo AR app on your mobile device and, keeping the cover in view, watch the augmented reality rise off the page. You can easily create similar augmented reality experiences for students using this app and others explored in this book.

Table 0.1. AR/VR tools used to enhance your experience of this book

APP	DESCRIPTION	IOS	GOOGLE PLAY
ARize bit.ly/ARize	Create AR online to view on a mobile device.		
ARLOOPA bit.ly/ARloopa	Create AR online to view on a mobile device.		
Assemblr bit.ly/AssemblR	Create AR online to view on a mobile device.		
AugmentifyIt bit.ly/AugmentifyIt	View AR on a mobile device.		

Introduction

CoSpaces cospaces.io/edu	Create and view AR on a mobile device.		
disruptED bit.ly/disruptedx	View AR & VR on a mobile device.		
EyeJack bit.ly/Eyejack	Create AR online to view on a mobile device.		
Flipgrid bit.ly/flipgridAr	View AR on a mobile device.		
Jig Workshop bit.ly/jigworkshop	Create AR-3D presentations online to view on a mobile device.		
Halo AR bit.ly/HaloAR	Create and view AR on a mobile device.		
MERGE Object Viewer bit.ly/ merge3Dobject	View and upload 3D content in the MERGE cube.		
Metaverse bit.ly/MetaverseAR	Create AR & VR online to view on a mobile device.		
NarratorAR bit.ly/narratorar	View AR on a mobile device.		

1 Benefits of Immersive Technology in Education

For those unfamiliar with the term, "immersive technology" refers to tools that incorporate augmented, virtual, and mixed reality. If you aren't quite sure what those terms mean, or if you're having trouble telling them apart, here are brief descriptions of each.

> In **augmented reaily** (**AR**), students can explore the real world while adding a digital layer on top that gives the illusion that they have a 3D object—like the solar system, a zebra, or a human cadaver—in their classroom.
>
> In **virtual reality** (**VR**), your classroom can teleport anywhere—to the Great Barrier Reef or ancient Rome—using a VR headset or mobile device to create an all-digital view. VR features such as a 360-degree view and surround sound provide a truly immersive experience.
>
> In **mixed reality** (**MR**), the AR experience goes beyond an overlay to allow virtual objects to interact with real ones, such as placing a virtual apple or skull on top of your real desk.

For the purposes of this book, I will use the terms "immersive technology" or "AR/VR." Some of the tools we will explore cross over into MR but as AR and VR are more commonly used, I will refer to all as "AR/VR."

Since one of the benefits of immersive technology is engagement, it's better to show than tell. Figure 1.1. shows examples of three different immersive technology experiences.

Benefits of Immersive Technology in Education

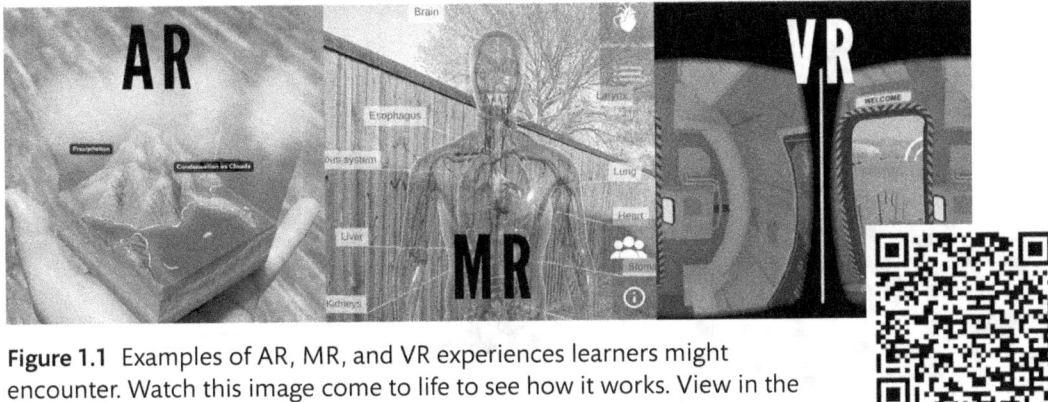

Figure 1.1 Examples of AR, MR, and VR experiences learners might encounter. Watch this image come to life to see how it works. View in the EyeJack app after scanning the QR code.

Now that you have a better picture of what these various technologies are, it's helpful to understand the kinds of opportunities they present and the benefits of using them with students before incorporating them into your classroom. This chapter explores the some of the advantages of using immersive technology in education, including:

- engagement
- investment
- flexibility
- challenge

Being aware of these benefits can help with planning as well as making the case for using the technology with administrators, parents, and others.

Student Engagement

The most obvious benefit of immersive technology is building student engagement. Most students are enthusiastic about trying this new technology; they've probably already been exposed to it through entertainment and gameplay. The "wow" factor of AR/VR will likely attract many students to classroom activities that they might normally dread. Suddenly, science content from lectures or reading assignments can come to life in a memorable way (see Figure 1.2). Using AR/VR tools, you are appealing to your students' desire to learn in a way that captures their attention and is more aligned with their time outside of school. When students don't think of learning as boring, you are more likely to fully engage them.

Figure 1.2. Use the AugmentifyIt app and scan each of these images. Capture the "wow" and share on social media using #ARVRinEDU.

The best engagement comes when the potential is unlimited. Our students need to encounter learning in multiple content areas and in many lessons. If the tool is limited to a single use, it may not be worth the time, cost, or resources. Spending an enormous amount of time preparing for an experience that is limited to just a single lesson may not be the best choice for you or your students.

Presenting on this topic has shown me that not only is it exciting for students, but educators widely accept it. Immersive technology offers a new way to present learning beyond our prior limitations. Educators across the globe are having just as much fun as their students and are reaping the many benefits, from increased engagment to deeper learning encounters. It's possible that immersive technology can spark a new enthusiasm for teaching as educators experience the fun with their students.

Not all people respond to various AR/VR experiences with enthusiasm. Some individuals are more comfortable with this technology than others. You may encounter situations that require some guidance or time to get buy-in for participation, especially when students are unsure how they might feel during the virtual experience. There are occasions when the experience of movement in VR can make students feel ill, uncomfortably claustrophobic, or vulnerable. Consider these possibilities before pressuring students into participating. One way to help students choose to join the experience is by preparing the class for the experience with a discussion in advance. You should also list the expectations for classroom behavior. Most students become willing to take the leap once they see other students enjoying the learning experience.

The following are a few ways to prepare for successful student participation when using immersive technology:

- Set specific objectives for the experience.
- List classroom behavior expectations.
- Provide detailed directions for device use.
- Prepare a safe place to explore learning, free of trip hazards or potential collisions with furniture.
- Balance student responsibility with interactions, responses, and assessments.
- Keep students active with age-appropriate transition times.

If you find that students are resisting the experience, try to provide alternative options until your students are comfortable with the activities. Some of the ways to supplement immersive technology lessons could include having students do a virtual scavenger hunt on the computer, use a mobile app that doesn't require a headset, or read related content online or in a physical book.

Student Investment

Providing the best learning experience for each student begins with knowing them. When we want the best for our students, we find ways to support their struggles and magnify their strengths. We understand the different ways our students enjoy learning. We discard activities when our students don't improve, and research how to offer a better lesson next time. Adapting to this mindset isn't driven by recognition, approval, or gratitude. We continuously adapt because we care about our students.

Finding the right resources can be challenging, especially when some publishers and companies are pushing products that are mainly driven by profit rather than educational value. Because of the popularity of immersive technology, new tools and updates are being released constantly, which can be both beneficial and problematic for educators.

On the benefit side, resources covering almost every educational topic are already available to bring into your classroom. I often receive requests for tools that fit a specific need in the curriculum. I'm always amazed when I research the topic and find many resources covering specific concepts. The challenge is finding good quality and the right fit among the scores of offerings.

While any topic you search for may be available in AR/VR, the results won't always match your or your students' expectations for learning. Sometimes the lesson doesn't need to be in AR/VR, and forcing the tool for the enjoyment of the activity alone is not the way to use any technology. Replacing a paragraph of text on a sheet of paper with a paragraph of text in a virtual space is unnecessary and a disappointing experience for students.

Careful evaluation of your lesson plan elements will help you select the right tools. Many lessons allow students to explore and interact with the concepts. If the lesson requires authentic audience feedback, immersive technology can provide these opportunities. AR/VR tools can provide virtual objects without spending a fortune on classroom materials. Many experiences provide connections to education standards to address student learning while expanding and improving your lesson plans with immersive technology.

Flexibility

While working with schools across the United States, a common trend I've found is district-created lesson plans and activities that must be strictly followed by educators. I'm always amazed when I'm invited to speak in a district that has such strict regulations on their teachers' options. The lessons that my sessions include seem to reopen old wounds. The discussion around what could be is a reminder of what is impossible for their classrooms because of district restrictions.

I understand the desire to use the same lessons from one campus to another. The uniform approach seems to be the right direction for districts trying to provide a quality education that has the research and testing for proven results. Each assignment and activity is carefully crafted to cover every objective and standard perfectly. The curriculum is so good that district administrators wonder why they don't have better scores, higher performance, and district-wide academic recognition. If we have the lessons so perfected, what's the point of having an educator in the classroom at all?

Of course, we all know that teaching involves more than strict guidelines, scripted lessons, and rigid activities. The educator has the opportunity to serve a diverse group of individuals that will respond to various lessons differently. Educators need to have the freedom to modify a lesson that won't fit each of our individual learners. One of the many rewards of being an educator is identifying the struggles of our students and seeing the success of finding the right approach to meet their individual needs. The challenge is gladly accepted because the teacher is hired to serve our students using effective strategies, not to follow a command that has a specific outcome every time it's repeated.

While teaching in the classroom, I couldn't give the exact same lesson in the same way from class to class. Delivering the same "speech" in each class was exhausting and to be honest, horribly dull. I found that I needed to be engaged in the material as much as the students needed it. Our students can see right through a phony act, and I'm a bad actress. If I wasn't engaged, how could I expect my students to be involved? It didn't take long to realize that I needed to add variety in my lessons that were modified from class to class. The difficulty of finding the right way to present material to each student was a challenge, but the results were what kept me excited about teaching.

Our students expect to be valued, just as educators expect to be appreciated. Our individual needs must be acknowledged and heard to feel valued. We must understand our students' difficulties and interests to create successful lessons. By modifying our lessons to fit their needs and interests, our students will feel valued and find greater success in their learning. Lessons can only be modified if the district values the decisions of our educators to make those changes.

In addition to personal preference, lessons must be flexible to fit our diverse learners. Meeting the needs of a student with dyslexia looks different than for a student who is visually impaired. There are many options to experience learning differently as immersive technology can get our students up and moving around the classroom, listening and watching biographies in 360 degrees, or creating a space that fits their individual interests. AR/VR tools provide flexibility for students to express their knowledge in ways that holistically display their understanding of content.

Student Challenge

Many classrooms have incorporated gamification and challenge-based activities such as Breakout EDU, eSports, badging, and others. Students are often captivated by the challenge to be successful under the constraints of competition and time.

Some of the most impressive immersive technology resources push users to make quick decisions, overcome obstacles, and persist until they reach their goal. Many students prefer some amount of struggle before finishing a task because the reward is much more meaningful after having to work hard. In the same way, educators can find great pleasure in "gamifying" AR/VR using challenges.

A Success Story with AR/VR from My Own Life

The chance to make mistakes while learning can help support long term retention and a deeper understanding of the content. Many times, we learn more from our failures than we do with immediate success. I've personally witnessed this to be true in my own family using an app called Catchy Words AR.

One evening, my daughter Elliana was struggling with spelling words, and my traditional "drill and kill" practices were not helping her. She would say each letter of the word over and over and write it down on a sheet of paper while looking back at the correct spelling. Elliana has dyslexia, so this frustration is nothing new, but we were finding that her spelling words were becoming more demanding and difficult for her to retain.

When the Catchy Words AR app was first released, I discounted it as nothing more than Hangman in AR. I couldn't clearly see the potential of the game, but when I noticed that Elli was struggling with these words, I thought I would have her give it a try. I typed in the letters of the word she was having the most difficulty with and gave her the device. The screen showed a 3D bubble in the middle of the room that held all of the letters of her spelling word. She had to walk up to the bubble with the device and tap it. Once she tapped the bubble with the device, all of the letters flew out and landed helter-skelter around the room. She had to collect each of these letters with the device and place it in the correct order in the boxes shown at the bottom of the room (see Figure 1.3).

Figure 1.3. Catchy Words AR experience. View this image using the Halo AR app to see the Catchy Words AR app in action.

Initially, I was optimistic that she would at the very least enjoy the activity, even if it didn't impact her academically. I didn't anticipate how long it would take her to complete the task. She struggled to look at the 3D letters all twisted and turned and strewn about the room. She would look from the right and then walk around to the left to identify and make sense of each of the letters. Her next hurdle was placing the letters in the boxes in the correct position. She would place the letters in the wrong space and then need to move the letter to the correct position.

In the background, I was biting my nails off. Why was this taking her so long? At her age, she should be able to run with this activity much quicker than I could, so what was the holdup? I was at my wits' end when she finally completed the activity successfully. The screen filled with confetti and you could hear clapping and cheers as the app celebrated her accomplishment.

I asked her how to spell the word. She told me! I was surprised but didn't get too overjoyed, as she had just finished the activity. An hour later I asked again, and she was still able to correctly spell the word. At this point, I was impressed that she was able to retain the information for that amount of time. The next morning on the way to school, Elli was again able to say the correct spelling for that word. I couldn't believe it! I had to go back and question what made the difference for her that wasn't offered in the traditional methods used previously. The most obvious was the kinesthetic learning that took place when she physically had to walk up and around the space to "play" the game. The research behind physical activity and learning (showing, for example, that kids who are more active have improved focus and retention) has been around for a while, but our educational system seems to continue to be stuck in a seat throughout most of the day. (Abdelbary, 2017)

Another significant difference in this immersive technology tool was specifically beneficial to Elliana. The 3D letters were twisted and rotated around the room in 360 degrees. As she walked up to the letters, she took so much time because her brain was struggling to make sense of that letter. The level of difficulty was increased for her brain, and it showed with the time it took her to complete the task. If our brain has to work this hard for success, it's smart enough to know to hold on to that information for the future, so it doesn't have to work that hard again. One of the benefits we have in our classrooms today is the easy access to information, but with all that information available, we have a more difficult time retaining because we didn't have to work as hard to find it. We can easily see an example of that in our own lives when we don't need to remember phone numbers any longer.

I later learned from an educator in one of my sessions that she had read that students with dyslexia learn best in 3D. While the research is still in process, the visual-spatial aspect appears to be very helpful. According to an article in the journal *The Dyslexic Reader*,

> Concepts are quickly comprehended when they are presented within a context and related to other concepts. Once spatial learners create a mental picture of a concept and see how the information fits with what they already know, their learning is permanent. Repetition is completely unnecessary and irrelevant to their learning style. (Silverman and Freed, 1991)

I wondered how many other students could also benefit from this type of learning. The experience also taught me how to avoid unnecessary and damaging ways to teach Elli.

Our classroom activities can include AR/VR challenges that stretch our students' knowledge, help them retain and understand information, and even identify personal learning needs; this might not be possible otherwise.

As you evaluate the benefits of immersive technology for your classroom, consider the interests, needs, and motivations of your students. The classroom environment should be full of opportunities for all learners and the motivation to bring these tools into your lessons is driven by your interest and investment in your students' success. The challenges that some educators and students may face to adopt these current technologies can often be solved through diligent support, encouragement, and modifications. Participate in the joy of learning with your students as you investigate and launch these resources throughout your lesson plans.

Immersive Learning Challenge

Ask your students to complete this questionnaire to identify their needs, wants, and interests around immersive technology.

1. On a scale of 1–5, circle the number that identifies how comfortable you are with using immersive technology (1 being the least and 5 being the most). It's also acceptable to say, "Don't know." 1   2   3   4   5

2. What are your past experiences using immersive technology (if any)?

3. Do you have any hesitations about using immersive technology? If so, why?

4. What skills do you plan to expand when using immersive technology in our lessons?

5. What is one thing you want me to know about using immersive technology in the classroom?

6. Are you interested in helping others understand how to use immersive technology? How?

How to Use Immersive Technology to Personalize Learning

Preparing to personalize the immersive technology tools to fit your student needs is challenging and requires time, research and sometimes, funding to meet each of their individual needs. In addition to identifying our students' needs, we need to research the right tools to meet their needs. When creating an opportunity for all students to receive the benefit of immersive technology, accessibility will impact a big role for some of our students. Understanding your students' needs and abilities will help determine the best immersive technology tools to include in your lesson plans.

Immersive technology should not be reserved for only our most tech-savvy teachers. Motivation, planning, and purpose will play a major role in the success of these tools, especially for the newbie. While fear of using new tools is a potential problem when adopting any technology, it can be mitigated through preparation. Does the educator have the dedication to carefully select the right tools? Has the educator planned out how to meet the individual needs of the students? Is there a reasonable goal to reach at the end of the lesson(s)? These questions are important when using immersive technology to avoid an ineffective lesson that doesn't provide any educational value.

This chapter shares questions and considerations that should inform decisions around immersive technology tools for your classroom.

Identify Areas of Need

I believe most educators are ready to embrace immersive technology, but they typically want a step-by-step process to get started. Trying something new is scary for some and having specific directions can bring the confidence necessary to give it a shot.

In nearly every presentation I provide on this topic, someone always asks me what app everyone should download. The problem with this question is that there is no one app for everyone. There isn't a perfect tool for every classroom or every student. The best approach to take when jumping into immersive technology for the first time is to have a specific need and goal. Below are some questions you should ask yourself.

Where are my students struggling?

The first question I often ask is what is my objective? What is the main purpose of using this kind of technology, and what would success look like? Identify where your students have gaps in learning and areas where you've been less than successful in the past. Find the tools that will support your struggling learners with the concepts that remain difficult to explain with words, text, or 2D pictures.

What do my students need to understand more deeply?

Providing students with the time to dig deep into a concept can give them foundational knowledge critical for learning new material. Individualized exploration within AR/VR can inspire passion and interest in topics that students might otherwise find boring, especially when taught using traditional methods. Time zones may seem difficult to grasp when looking at a picture of a map, but when a student connects with another student in a far-away country using VR, the concept of time zone differences becomes more relatable. Viewing the earth orbiting the sun in 3D in AR allows the student to walk around the solar system and see multiple perspectives: planet rotations, planet orbits, how eclipses happen. Providing personal experiences and new ways of seeing systems are just a couple advantages of lessons using AR/VR.

Some content is hard to bring into the classroom without AR/VR. Many times, our students need to learn about a concept that is difficult to visit or too dangerous to explore. A lesson on the coral reef ecosystem would be difficult for a classroom to observe in person or exploring the moon's three main landforms would be unimaginable to see without the use of technology. Use immersive technology resources to bypass those restrictions and limitations!

What Immersive Technology Is Right for Your School?

In a conversation with an administrator a few years back, she shared her interest in implementing virtual reality in her school district. I was asked what VR viewer the school should purchase. At this time, the school was looking for a cheap option similar to Google Cardboard where a mobile device would slide into a viewer. To make the right recommendation, I asked what devices the school had to put in the viewers. The administrator was stumped because she didn't know they needed to make a purchase beyond the viewers. It was obvious that she needed more help than just selecting the right VR viewer.

As the conversation progressed I was able to learn more about the district's needs, available devices, and their specific interest in using the technology. A discussion of campus technical support was important, because she didn't realize that training on the specific resources would be necessary for the teachers to successfully use the tools.

The most important part of the discussion was regarding the needs of the students. I was informed that the tools weren't for the general classroom in this case, but for the gifted and talented classrooms. Based on her responses, I recommended a purchase plus teacher training that targeted the specific needs of those students. All of these questions are important to discuss before moving forward with implementing AR/VR—or any technology for that matter.

In most cases, I typically recommend educators begin using immersive technology with the devices they already have available. A common misunderstanding educators have is that they need to have a big budget to begin using AR/VR. I urge educators to begin using the technology on the device they already have in their classroom.

AR/VR Offers Accessibility

The learning opportunities provided by AR/VR can be especially beneficial to students with physical limitations. I've listed some important factors to consider when making immersive technology purchases that provide access and opportunity for all students.

AR/VR Accessibility Checklist

Consider the following features of AR/VR tools to ensure they are accessible for all students.

Mobility

- Does the tool require physical movement?
- Is the student required to view the entire 360-degree scene (i.e., will the student need to turn around)?
- Is there a height requirement (selecting or grabbing objects at standing height)?
- Does the experience create motion sickness? How does your student tolerate motion sickness?

Interactions

- Does the remote work with your students' abilities?
- How does the user manipulate the experience?
- Are there multiple options to engage in the experience, such as: gaze to select, speak to select, hand tracking, etc.?

Visual

- Are there options to customize the clarity of the view with adjustable lenses?
- Can the text be modified in size, color, contrast, font type, brightness, or spacing?
- Is the scene adjustable in location?

Auditory

- Is spatialized audio included to give an AR experience, even without the visual requirement?
- Does the experience allow for headphones?
- Can the student feel vibration or resistance through haptic feedback?

A Success Story with AR/VR from My Own Life

I once visited family on Thanksgiving, including an extended family that I'd never met before. When I first arrived, I was quickly introduced to the new family, including Trace, a fourteen-year-old boy. Trace was born with arthrogryposis and is unable to control his fingers. He is limited in mobility and has to use a wheelchair to get around. Despite these challenges, I soon learned that Trace is extremely talented.

Trace has found a way to overcome his limitations by using his feet to hold, control, and manage items. I was amazed when his mother shared that he was able to use a bow and arrow with his feet.

I try to bring out my immersive technology devices during the holidays for the children in the family. That year, I was able to bring my Oculus Quest, Oculus Go, and Samsung Odyssey so the children could play in VR. The Quest and the Go are both standalone devices, so they don't need to be hooked up to a computer in order to experience VR. I first asked Trace if he was interested in trying out VR. He and his mother agreed that he could. He shared that he had never seen VR before, and that his school didn't have anything like it.

Considering his specific needs, I understood that the device ought to be limited to a single remote (not dual), and stationary (not requiring walking around). I immediately knew that the Oculus Go was the right device for him. Since the Oculus Quest has more functionality than the Go, I rarely recommend the Go, but in this case the technology limitations were not the focus, the needs of the child were.

I supported Trace to get the headset on, and when I handed him the controller, I was shocked how quickly he was able to figure out the remote using his feet. He started scrolling through the

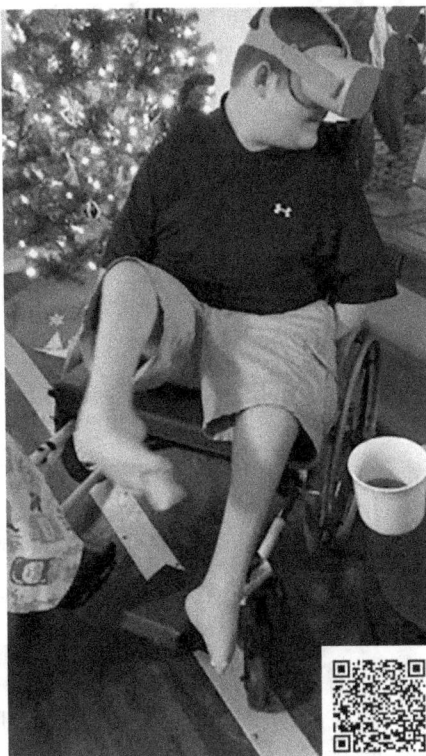

Figure 2.1. Trace using the Oculus Go. Open the EyeJack app and scan the QR code to see the video.

library of apps and began his first experience by going to the moon using the Apollo 11 app. The scene begins by placing the user in a typical 1960s living room, watching a TV give announcements of the upcoming launch. Following that scene, the user is brought into the Apollo 11 spacecraft and launched from Earth, eventually landing on the moon.

The laughter and joy coming from Trace during the VR experience made all of us standing around giggle with happiness (see Figure 2.1). Trace explored a few more apps before finally taking off the headset due to low battery. After, I asked Trace some questions about the VR experience in the Oculus Go.

Trace found his favorite app in the headset to be the rollercoaster app. Normally, I recommend that users avoid the rollercoasters, because they typically feel sick within the first few minutes from all the motion. What I didn't consider with Trace is that he had never been able to ride a rollercoaster in his life. I realized that this technology was giving Trace a sensation of mobility that he had never had before.

When I asked Trace if he thought this technology should be at his school, he said he thought it was a better way to learn. He explained that he struggles to remember what he's reading, but that he would never forget his VR experiences. I believe many of our students can relate to Trace, even those without a disability.

While one device or app may be commonly recommended more than another, you need to consider your students first. If I had put the Oculus Quest on Trace, the requirement to stand up and walk around using two remotes would have made the experience a complete disaster. He would have struggled to align two controllers, and he would have had a difficult time turning around to face the various scenes.

I was impressed with how adaptable the VR headset was to be utilized by a person with physical limitations. The encounter with Trace was a reminder that each of our students deserves the chance to learn with immersive experiences.

 ## Immersive Learning Challenge

Ask students to create a list of AR/VR resources that they prefer to use and why. Ask them to explain what limitations they may have and to also consider what resources might work for students of all abilities.

App Hacking

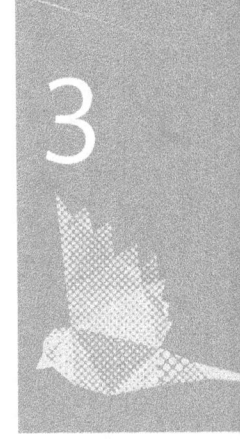

Many immersive technology tools are created with a specific objective for the classroom; however, the most useful tools are flexible enough to fit the needs and interests of all students. Some tools may at first seem to offer exactly what we need, but students will easily find limitations and restrictions they want to "hack" to allow more access and flexibility. Our students are capable of finding ways to "unlock" technology tools now more than ever before.

We are constantly provided with a million ways to use Google products, and most of those strategies originated from users, not from the company that created the tool. Similarly, most AR/VR apps are made with a specific intention for use, but that doesn't mean that our students have to be restricted to only the intended usage. Don't view "app hacking" as a problem for the teacher to solve, but rather as an opportunity for students to use their problem-solving capabilities.

I work with startup companies as often as I work with educators, and this has provided me with many opportunities to collaborate and make product recommendations. There is always room for improvement, updates, new features, and new functionalities. One advantage of immersive technology is how quickly it's growing and offering an abundance of resources for diverse learners. The growth is happening so rapidly that there's often not enough time for publishers to make all the necessary adjustments before publication, so it's up to users—including educators and students—to maximize these tools.

Push the Limits of Tools to Find New Capabilities

Have you ever crashed an app because you pushed the tool beyond what it could handle? Examples include adding too many library items, too many slides, too many graphics, or too much of anything to overload the app so that it freezes or shuts down. I run into this problem often, because I enjoy the challenge of seeing how far I can go, or because I'm curious to see if the developer thought ahead to prepare for a particular situation. I can identify with students who, when trying new technologies, don't listen to instructions and jump in headfirst without a plan for where they're going or where they'll arrive. Some of the fun can be found in the unknown and in stretching an app's capabilities.

On the other hand, some students seriously struggle to do anything without step-by-step instructions. I've found this especially true when working with gifted and talented students. The struggle begins when these students are given open assignments without clearly identifying the exact product at the end. The best AR/VR tools don't limit you to a final product that looks like everyone else's. In some ways, immersive technology reminds me of giving a student a crayon and asking them what's possible. Asking students to explore the limits of these tools may cause them discomfort at first, but as they gain more confidence from success and learn from failure, they will begin testing boundaries.

Before letting students loose in immersive technology, prepare them for what they should learn. When they know their specific learning objectives using AR/VR, they are more likely to achieve them. In addition, evaluating what they learned helps you know which direction to go next.

Nearpod App Hacking Example

One example of app hacking involved a presentation I delivered with my good friend Rachelle Dene Poth. In our presentation, we talked about making Nearpod work for our goals of sharing immersive technology. Nearpod is an interactive presentation platform that allows students to engage in activities, games, and VR experiences in their classroom lessons. The educator is able to create engaging lessons by delivering content in a visually appealing way and also receiving student responses in real time. The AR and VR options to create content in Nearpod may seem limited, but I've found some of the integrations allow for creative use.

After a little brainstorming with Rachelle, we found many other tools that could be incorporated into Nearpod by adding web content to specific slides. The Nearpod option to bring in more tools through web content was not necessarily intended for immersive experiences, so we tested dozens of sites to see what functionality was available within the Nearpod slides. We also checked both mobile and desktop platforms to see what restrictions the user might run into.

Figure 3.1. Access our Hacking Nearpod presentation at tiny.cc/hackingnearpod.

Many immersive technology tools don't involve student responses, which is why hacking Nearpod was important. The resources and experiences in immersive technology are incredible, but we can't assume that students understood and retained every part of the experience because it was in 3D or 360 degrees.

I'm a huge advocate of web-based AR/VR (webXR), especially for our classrooms, so the connection to these resources fits perfectly in the Nearpod platform. In Nearpod, students can create, view, and experience various AR/VR tools while also responding and collaborating at the same time.

The QR code for Figure 3.1 takes you the Hacking Nearpod presentation Rachelle and I created. Among the tools that you'll find in the presentation are CoSpaces, Google Poly, Google Street View, YouTube, and RoundMe. Several of these will be featured in the next chapter, when I discuss app smashing.

WallaMe App Hacking Example

In the past, I've used an app called WallaMe to create and share AR scavenger hunts. This location-based AR messaging app allows individuals to leave public or private messages for people that arrive in a specific place. Imagine sending a text message to your friend, who can't receive the message until he arrives at a certain spot and scans the right object to see the message. Your friend will find the object and hover his device over it to see the secret message appear on top using augmented reality.

Messages can also be public, so that anyone with WallaMe can see them in AR. The anticipation of receiving the message after searching for the right location adds to the enjoyment and creativity of messaging.

The WallaMe app isn't intended to be used for scavenger hunts, but I use the tool in this way because it works with both iOS and Android devices. I set up challenge messages in various locations and tether them to an object in each place. Sometimes I use my own printed-out images, and other times I connect the AR to artwork on the wall. I leave the challenge in an AR message, and the person participating in the scavenger hunt must accomplish the task before moving on to the next location.

Since the WallaMe app is not intended for scavenger hunts, it takes some explaining during my professional development sessions before I send attendees out to find the AR challenges. I first demonstrate finding the AR within the app by mirroring my device on a projector. I then send the groups out to participate in the scavenger hunt. When the hunt is over, the attendees can then create their own AR messages to leave around the room. Hacking the WallaMe app has allowed more teachers to participate in the scavenger hunts since it works with both iOS and Android devices.

Easy Steps to Create Hidden Messages with the WallaMe App

7. Download the WallaMe app from the App Store or Google Play and create an account.
8. Select the + button.
9. Take a picture of an image.
10. Add a photo, text, or drawing on top of the picture, select the green checkmark in the top right corner, then the white arrow.
11. Make the AR message visible to the public, or turn it off and select a particular contact to share it with.
12. Confirm by selecting the white arrow at the bottom of the screen.

EyeJack App Hacking Example

Another tool used for creating AR content is EyeJack. The EyeJack app is designed to bring artwork to life with an AR overlay. I've hacked EyeJack by using it for more purposes than it was intended for. One of the uses I've found for EyeJack is creating promotional material. I created a postcard about #ARVRinEDU and shared it with educators at events so they can see AR come to life in their hands (Figure 3.2).

EyeJack can be hacked to layer AR on top of clothing, books, cards, sketchnotes, and more. Students will find many ways to turn any still image into AR media. Similar to WallaMe, EyeJack can also be used for an interactive scavenger hunt by layering videos rather than messages.

> **Easy Steps to Create with EyeJack**
>
> 1. Download the EyeJack app on your computer.
> 2. Upload a trigger image (JPG or PNG file).
> 3. Upload a video, GIF, or PNG to layer on top of the trigger image in the augmented reality experience.
> 4. Keep the QR code pulled up in order to scan with the mobile app.
> 5. Download the EyeJack app on your mobile device (iOS or Android).
> 6. Open the app and select the eye at the bottom of the screen. Scan the QR code (found in step 4) and view the trigger image using EyeJack.

Figure 3.2. View my postcard using the EyeJack app after scanning the QR code above. You'll see a video that I layered on top in AR.

Share Ideas with Immersive Technology Companies

As immersive technology continues to captivate the education space, it's worth your while to connect with app creators to share your app hacking ideas, or suggestions for improvement. One advantage of immersive technology companies compared to others is their interest in hearing from teachers and students. Companies may have great concepts but lack understanding of how to effectively implement their products for classroom use. The opportunity to influence the tools for your classroom is powerful, as other classrooms can benefit when you share feedback.

The best way to reach these companies is by connecting through social media. Table 3.1 lists the Twitter handles of some immersive technology. Allow your classroom to have a voice in future products by sharing the hacks your students made. Don't forget to include #ARVRinEDU in your posts to connect with and inspire the larger community.

Table 3.1. AR/VR companies and how to find them on Twitter

COMPANY	HANDLE	COMPANY	HANDLE
ANIMA RES	@animares	**MEL Science**	@mel_science
ARVRinEDU	@ARVRinEDU	**Metaverse**	@MetaverseApp
AstroReality	@AstroRealityAR	**Minecraft Earth**	@minecraftearth
AugmentifyIt	@AugmentifyIt	**MergeEDU**	@mergeedu
Catchy Words AR	@CatchyWordsApp	**Moatboat**	@moatboat
ClassImmerse	@LearnrollCenter	**Mozilla Hubs**	@MozillaHubs
ClassXR	@ClassXr	**Narrator AR**	@NarratorAR
CoSpaces	@CoSpaces_Edu	**Nearpod**	@nearpod
Curiscope	@curiscope	**Oculus**	@oculus
disruptED	@disrupted_x	**Qlone**	@QloneApp
DrawmaticAR	@DrawmaticAR	**QuantumERA**	@QuantumERA
EON Reality	@EONRealityInc	**ScavengarEDU**	@ScavengarEDU

COMPANY	HANDLE	COMPANY	HANDLE
Explore Interactive	@ExploreARplay	**Torch AR**	@torchapp
EyeJack	@eyejackapp	**Thyng**	@ThyngApp
Gravity Sketch	@GravitySketch	**VictoryXR**	@VictoryXR_VR_AR
Kai's Clan	@kais_clan	**VirtualSpeech**	@vrspeech
LightUp	@lightup	**Wonderscope**	@WonderscopeApp
Magicplan	@Magic_Plan	**ZoeXR**	@ZoeXR

 ## Immersive Learning Challenge

What can your students create in WallaMe or EyeJack? Create a new way to use these tools by layering AR on top of classwork, images, artwork, or projects. Share your ideas on social media using #ARVRinEDU.

4 App Smashing

Our educational system is full of innovation. When we don't have the right supplies, we creatively use what we have to accomplish the same goal. When we get a new student who's behind, we find a way to fit in additional teaching to catch them up. When we have an unexpected remote learning semester, we find a way to check on each of our students to offer encouragement and support. I'm always amazed at how educators can adapt to offer the best for students.

Finding ways to make immersive technology tools work for students can be a challenge. Tools often have a specific purpose and don't always fit the needs of every student. Using multiple resources for one project is common as they can offer different purposes and benefits. One way to make multiple tools work better for your students is by combining the tools together. This process of combining two or more apps to create a project or accomplish a task is called "app smashing."

An example of app smashing is using a camera app to capture photos, loading one of those photos into Canva to modify the image, then adding the modified image into the Google Slides app. The three different tools are used to create a larger project. Each tool plays its own role in optimizing the final product. The benefit of app smashing is making the tool fit the needs of your students instead of making your students adapt to the tool.

App Smashing in Action: Flipgrid and MERGE Explorer

Let's take a closer look at app smashing in the classroom with the combination of two popular apps, MERGE Explorer and Flipgrid. These tools are used for different purposes but, when combined, can support powerful student collaboration and reflection.

Many educators find Flipgrid to be an engaging, free video app that encourages student feedback and responses. Perhaps the greatest benefit of Flipgrid is the students' enthusiasm to share their stories in video format. The FlipgridAR feature allows students to respond via video and then receive a QR code to see the video in augmented reality. The video is revealed using the Flipgrid student app when scanning the QR code.

MERGE EDU products have made a huge splash in education by bringing 3D content to life in the palm of your hand using the MERGE Cube. The same MERGE Cube is used to explore and engage with classroom curriculum using a multitude of content cards. The integration of Microsoft's Immersive Reader allows students to read and see the content in their preferred color, font size, and language, among many other options. In addition to the text, students engage with the curriculum by dissecting, expanding, exploding, stretching, selecting, and more using the MERGE Cube.

As stated by Linda Edwards, a technology integration specialist in Toronto, "Some things just naturally go together like peanut butter and jam or bacon and eggs. That's the way I feel about MERGE VR and Flipgrid; they too are a perfect pairing." Edwards was able to app smash FlipgridAR with MERGE EDU Explorer. Using the MERGE Explorer app, students explored the life cycle of a frog. They were able to discover each cycle—from egg, to embryo, to tadpole, to frog. The final experience in the app is a frog dissection to explore each of the body parts. Each phase displays an animated 3D object while asking students to interact with and identify the parts of the frog (minus the formaldehyde). As students explore, they can easily record their experiences, which load onto the camera roll of the device.

The app smashing began when students took the recordings of their experiences in MERGE Explorer and uploaded the videos to Flipgrid in response to questions. The students were able to personalize their video in Flipgrid by adding emojis, using the whiteboard, and layering text on top of their videos.

The students were able to get instruction personalized for them through the Immersive Reader integration with MERGE Explorer while capturing their learning to share and collaborate with other students in Flipgrid. Students could respond to the uploaded videos and ask additional questions in Flipgrid. Explore the project and student responses by scanning the QR code in Figure 4.1.

Edwards felt these resources were especially important for her ELL and special needs students. These students were able to get individualized instruction by reading and listening to the text and interacting with the AR experience while explaining their knowledge on video, then hearing other students' responses via Flipgrid. The self-directed AR experiences allowed students to take ownership of their learning by setting their own accommodations and preferences. Edwards says, "Combining MERGE VR and FlipgridAR creates the magic! The Evidence of learning, the ability to share that learning, and the ability to provide timely feedback are a winning combination."

Figure 4.1. Scan the QR code to discover how Linda Edwards' students app smashed with MERGE Explorer and FlipgridAR. The experience is viewable using the EyeJack app.

Smashable Video Tools

There are many other AR apps that create videos which can be loaded into Flipgrid. FaceReplaced, PuppetMaster, YoPuppet, and LightUp are just a few. These AR apps create videos that load on your device and can then be app smashed with multiple applications. To understand how to create videos using these resources, learn more about the tools below.

FaceReplaced

FaceReplaced uses AR to add a character on top of your face, matching your expressions. The character can come from your camera roll or be captured in the app. The student syncs up the mouth, nose, and eyes to bring the character to life using the camera. Watch the FaceReplaced process by scanning Figure 4.2 in the Assemblr app.

App Smashing

Figure 4.2. View this image using the Assemblr app with the scan feature.

PuppetMaster

PuppetMaster uses a motion capture feature that tracks the body movement of an individual. Using the camera, the app identifies arm, leg, and head movements and replicates the same movement with a virtual puppet while recording the voice of the student. After the puppet is animated and the voice recording is combined, the student can add the video of the puppet to the camera roll of the device or to a background from the app library. Imagine building a character out of clay, having the clay character follow your movements, and recording the animation to your camera roll.

YoPuppet

Create an AR puppet show using YoPuppet! The app identifies your hand and synchronizes the selected puppet to match the movements of your hand—opening and shutting the mouth of the puppet. Videos can be shared or incorporated within other tools. Check out an example of a YoPuppet I created by scanning the QR code in Figure 4.3.

Figure 4.3. Scan the QR code using your camera to view a bird in 3D (using the myWebAR link). Tap the video to play.

App Smashing with AR Creation Tools

The benefit of app smashing goes beyond creating videos using AR. App smashing AR apps can combine 3D-created objects viewable in the palm of your hand with other activities or projects. Create an AR scavenger hunt, design scannable pages that come to life, or build a Minecraft castle in your playground. There are numerous ways to combine AR apps to support your curriculum.

Scanning 3D Objects with Qlone

One of the most impressive and consistent 3D scanning apps for your mobile device is Qlone (pronounced "clone"). This app provides a printable QR code to place a small item on and then guides the user to scan it from various angles to capture every part of the item. When the scan is complete, the user is able to export the resulting 3D virtual object in various file formats.

An important element when building AR/VR is using 3D assets to create the scene. The 3D objects created in Qlone can be uploaded into many AR apps, several of which are detailed below. While every app will have different file requirements, the most common file types for 3D objects when using them with AR/VR are STL, OBJ, FBX, GLB, and GLTF; some apps accept zip files as well.

QLONE AND COSPACES

A popular AR/VR creation tool is CoSpaces. Using CoSpaces, students can design, code, and customize AR/VR spaces that are viewable on the web (in VR) or through the CoSpaces app on a mobile device (AR and VR). CoSpaces is known for incredible immersive experiences that students can build, while also offering multiplatform and collaborative projects. Its customization includes the ability to upload 2D and 360-degree photos, audio files, GIFs, and 3D objects. Using Qlone, students can scan an object from the classroom or their home and upload the 3D object into a CoSpaces project to view in AR or VR.

QLONE AND MERGE OBJECT VIEWER

The MERGE Object Viewer app was the first MERGE app released with an emphasis on student creation. The app allows students to upload a 3D object and view it using the MERGE Cube. The 3D object can come from a scan in Qlone or be created using many other 3D creation platforms. Once the object is uploaded, MERGE provides a specific object code that allows others to view the same 3D file. Students can organize 3D files into collections and share them with others. You can easily stamp the objects into your AR/VR space to build your own 3D museum. Figure 4.4 demonstrates how 3D objects appear using a MERGE Cube.

QLONE AND MERGE AND COSPACES

At the ISTE conference in 2018, CoSpaces and MERGE announced a partnership to modify the MERGE Cube to incorporate AR. Within the CoSpaces platform, students have the option to drag and drop 3D objects on and around the MERGE Cube. Using scanned objects from Qlone, students can easily see, hold, and turn the objects in their hands with the MERGE Cube while also adding animated library items into the scene from CoSpaces.

Figure 4.4. View Ellie the Elephant in 3D using a MERGE Cube. Open the Object Viewer app, select "Code Search," and type in code YVV1LG.

QLONE AND THYNG

My most recommended resource for uploading 3D content is the Thyng app. Thyng offers a library of 3D objects to load into your AR space, but one of the best features for the classroom is the option to import your own 2D or 3D content. Export the 3D object from Qlone in OBJ, STL, or FBX format to import into Thyng. Thyng allows the student to place AR content on surfaces, or the content may be accessed through a trigger image that you scan. Keep in mind that many AR/VR tools incorporate low poly objects—meaning the quantity of polygons to create the object is limited to function best in various platforms—so scanned objects may not function as well.

QLONE AND ASSEMBLR

The Assemblr app provides many different AR experiences to explore. More than content consumption, the recent release of Assemblr Studio makes AR creation simple but flexible enough for additional interactions. Assemblr Studio is available to download as a desktop or mobile app. Add video or custom 3D FBX files from the Qlone app on top of the Assemblr QR code provided and watch the augmented reality magic come to life.

Reality Composer, Adobe Aero, Scavengar and Assemblr

A newer file format originally specific to Apple is the USDZ file format, which is becoming more and more accepted across other platforms. Apple released the Reality Composer app to create custom 3D scenes and animation viewable in AR. Around the same time, Adobe released its new Aero app that essentially does the same thing. Each app offers a small library of 3D content; both allow the import of custom 3D objects.

Scavengar is an incredible AR scavenger hunt app that takes students on a digital hunt in a specific location, even if that location is elsewhere. Initially, the app required users to be together in one specific location. An update now allows anyone to participate in the hunt, regardless of their location. The app scans the floor and sends the hunt geography to any participant, so they can play in their own space. The update is perfect timing for students who are learning remotely, as they can "hunt" in their own space.

Scavengar gives teachers and students the freedom to create customized AR scavenger hunts that offer engaging, active learning for any lesson. The app allows users to score points for the following: correct answers, collecting coins, leaving feedback, and the speed at which they complete the hunt. A new release includes the option to import customized 3D content (USDZ) into the hunt, including experiences created in Reality Composer or Adobe Aero. This is the first of many new features that will allow teachers to create personalized classroom or remote learning experiences.

Storyfab and EyeJack

Storyfab is an extremely versatile AR storytelling app. The app allows students to create AR stories, recording them scene by scene and capturing various viewpoints as the cameraman or woman. Each scene is set up in AR using a large library of assets, characters, expressions, and actions. The student directs the scene, speaks for the characters, modifies the props, changes the mood, and more—using Storyfab options while recording each part of the story. When the recording is complete, the video loads into the camera roll, ready to app smash with other tools. EyeJack is a perfect candidate. The first image of the recording can be the trigger image for EyeJack, while the full video can layer on top of that image.

App Smashing with VR

App smashing is not limited to just AR apps. There are numerous options for app smashing with VR. Using your own 360-degree images and videos, you can build incredible VR experiences and immersive projects by combining different apps together. Following are some examples of app smashing VR apps.

Street View

Did you know that your mobile device can capture 360-degree images for free? Street View is one of the most popular apps that can capture 360-degree images. The app works on most mobile devices. One of the most important features in any 360-degree camera app is the option to save the images into your camera roll. Apps that load images into their server don't give you the freedom to app smash.

The Street View app guides the user in capturing several images from many angles, and then stitches each image together to create a completed "sphere" of all the images. Upload the finalized 360-degree image into other VR applications, and the option to layer new objects on top of the image or build virtual tours becomes possible.

CoSpaces

In CoSpaces, students can upload 3D objects, sound files, images, videos, and 360-degree images. Upload a 360-degree image created in Street View to customize the background of your virtual space. Layer characters, animals, nature, and buildings on top of your 360-degree images to give the space multiple dimensions and make the scene feel more realistic.

RoundMe

There are numerous applications that load 360-degree images to display information in an immersive experience. RoundMe is a virtual tour creator that works within a browser or as a mobile app and offers some great features. The virtual tours feature interactive portals, hotspots of information, directional sound, and shareable links and embed codes. Students can import 360-degree images captured in Street View into the RoundMe website to build beautiful, customized, virtual tours.

Tour Creator and Google Earth Projects

Google has built a foundation for an immersive library of users created 360-degree images, virtual reality tours, and 3D content. Google Poly includes the popular Tour Creator app to build custom VR tours using 360-degree images from Google Maps. Students can upload their personal 360-degree images created in Street View and easily build virtual reality tours. The option to add 360-degree images from the map is available if needed. Each tour allows for ambient sound, hotspots of information, and a sharable link to invite others to view. The personalized VR tours can be app smashed with Google Expeditions when using the same Google account.

Unfortunately, Tour Creator and the Expeditions app weren't as popular as expected; Google announced the products would be discontinued in June of 2021. Many of the resources will move to the Google Arts & Culture app, where users can continue enjoying the VR experiences. For building immersive tours, Google Earth Projects is now a creation platform incorporating 3D maps, text, personal images and videos.

In Google Earth Projects, students can create a customized 2D, 3D, or 360-degree view. The projects can include text boxes to list important information in the map view. In addition to text, the tour can contain customized lines to show paths or boundaries on a map to deepen storytelling in the presentation. The tour is located in Google Drive and allows for multiple collaborators to edit the map. Sharing the tour is as simple as sharing a link, similar to sharing a Google Doc. The integration of Google Maps and Street View provides access to numerous 360-degree content to make the project specific to the needs of the student. Google Earth Projects delivers a more customizable tour creation option for the classroom and I anticipate there will be much more to come.

Nearpod

Nearpod is an incredible, interactive tool that allows students to actively participate in presentations through feedback, drawing, assessment, collaboration, and more. My favorite feature in the Nearpod platform is the VR tours. The 360-degree images are connected to the 360cities.com library, which allows the user to easily bring VR into any Nearpod lesson. You can easily lead your own VR tour—created in RoundMe or Google Earth Projects—by bringing the students to a website within the lesson.

In addition to 360-degree content, Nearpod allows app smashing with 3D objects. Upload your own 3D objects into Google Poly, then add them into Nearpod lessons using links. Sketchfab is another popular 3D content library that can be used to add objects into lessons using links.

Oculus Quest

Oculus recently released two standalone devices that have begun to make high-end VR devices available to the average consumer. The first release was the Oculus Go (mentioned in Chapter 2 with the example of Trace), but Oculus has recently announced support will soon no longer be available for this device as more enthusiasm is now directed towards their latest VR headset, the Oculus Quest. Oculus

Quest is one of my favorite headsets because it gives students the freedom to walk around and interact within their space. The device uses front-facing cameras to track movement, and the user has two remotes to interact within the platform. The Oculus Quest is a standalone device that doesn't require a separate computer connected by a cord, wifi, or bluetooth.

The Quest is quite affordable, which is why it continues to stand out from other high-end VR devices; unfortunately, it lacks management for schools and is currently limited to ages thirteen and up. For those students who can benefit from this device, there are incredible creation tools to discover. A few of the possibilities for app smashing with Oculus Quest are mentioned below.

Tilt Brush

Google Tilt Brush has been around for a little while but is only available on specific (more high-end) VR devices. Using the Oculus Quest, students can use Tilt Brush to design 3D artwork. When beginning to draw in 3D, most people begin drawing items that are flat. Creating 3D artwork in VR has a bit of a learning curve, but has great potential for students' creative expression. After creating artwork, students can publish their work to Google Poly, where the 3D objects will be available online to app smash with many other applications.

Zoe

A newer creation app available on the Oculus Quest is Zoe. The company has brought coding with Unity and VR designs together in this app, making it possible to code with the Unity plugin and create conditions and interactions within the VR platform. Zoe allows students to upload 3D content into the virtual space. Using Qlone, students can scan their own objects and load them into the Google Poly library, which is integrated with Zoe, to bring into their VR space.

An additional benefit of creating in Zoe is collaboration and creating in groups. Students can work together to build VR spaces. Zoe has a new mobile application that works with the VR platform to allow multiple students on various devices to collaborate and create together.

Virtual Meeting Spaces

A new way to connect online is through VR in the browser. Using AR or VR through the browser is referred to as WebXR. (Learn more about WebXR in Chapter 5.) The flexibility to use immersive technology through a browser eliminates the limitations of downloading apps. There are several platforms for creating VR meeting spaces, many of which can be customized for you and your students through app smashing.

Mozilla Hubs and Spoke (and 3D objects from Qlone)

Mozilla has created an online VR resource called Hubs. The Hubs platform connects people online in a 360-degree space using mobile devices, tablets, computers, or VR headsets.

Designing the VR space in Hubs is simple. App smashing with Spoke delivers a flexible, customized VR space that can be designed and published immediately before inviting others to join in the space. Customize a classroom to meet on a boat in the ocean, garden, or stadium. There are no limits to app smashing with Spoke to design the perfect meeting space for your students.

Hubs is also connected to a few 3D object libraries including Google Poly. Uploading your own 3D content is possible, but often a better option is searching for a particular 3D object through the integrated libraries. You can explore a virtual space that I created in Hubs (see Figure 4.5).

Figure 4.5. Explore my Hubs VR space by going to hub.link/CdRBdXU.

FrameVR.io

Another WebXR resource for virtual meetings is FrameVR.io. This site allows users to connect, collaborate, and draw and upload 3D objects into the space. The FrameVR.io site also works with mobile devices, tablets, computers, and VR headsets. Similar to Hubs, in FrameVR.io students can upload 3D objects to discuss and share with other classmates.

Combined AR and VR Examples

In many cases, app smashing AR and VR apps together can bring the best of both worlds to your classroom. AR and VR app smashing can build portals, create immersive lessons, or customize virtual meeting spaces.

Gravity Sketch and Object Viewer

Similar to Google Tilt Brush, another favorite creation tool to draw and design artwork in 3D is Gravity Sketch. In Oculus Quest, the drawing tools seem to be more intuitive than in Tilt Brush, and more importantly, the export feature to save 3D artwork is more straightforward. When the object is available on a computer, the Merge Object Viewer app is a fantastic way to visualize 3D content. App smashing Gravity Sketch with the Object Viewer app allows you to view and stamp your 3D creations made in VR into your physical space using AR.

Figment AR

The Figment AR app is an AR tool that layers animated characters and portals in your space. The animated characters are 3D emojis. The AR portal looks like a window floating in your room, but when you go through the window with your mobile device, you enter a 360-degree experience. There are a few 360-degree experiences loaded in the app, but one of the best features is the option to upload your own 360-degree image or video. Using the Street View apps, students can import their own 360-degree images from their camera roll into the app and allow others to enter their VR experience.

RemixVR

The RemixVR website is an immersive resource that allows you to customize lessons to include 3D objects and 360-degree videos or images in a lesson plan. Imagine creating a lesson in Nearpod, but instead of viewing slides, students join the lesson and, using AR portals, enter the 360-degree images you upload. Each student can join and independently experience the lesson on their own device at any location. App smash with Qlone by uploading 3D objects into the space. This tool is perfect for remote classrooms as students don't have to be physically present to participate.

Metaverse and Street View

The Metaverse application is a massive immersive technology resource for education. The application is able to customize experiences using both AR and VR, questions, polls, pictures, and so much more. Using Metaverse, educators and students build AR/VR experiences that can gather results, provide information, create leaderboards, set timers, and collect points, among other possibilities.

In Metaverse, AR portals and scenes use 360-degree images uploaded by the user. Another app smashing option is using customized 3D objects with Google Poly integration. Students can see 3D objects placed in their real world with augmented reality. View my experience below by scanning the QR code.

Kai's Clan and Tinkercad

Kai's Clan is one of the most impressive robotics, coding, and immersive technology sets I've come across. The program is accessible online and requires compatible robots and mats as well as a mobile stand. Using your computer and mobile device, the robots are coded to move and navigate on the mat. The mats contain various experiences that come to life in augmented reality. In VR mode, the students see the robot's view of the scene (see Figure 4.6).

The app smashing possibility with Kai's Clan is loading 3D objects. An integration with Tinkercad is available on the Kai's Clan platform: the user can upload 3D content on the creator mat or customize the look of the robots. The use of both AR and VR gives students different perspectives and makes coding a relatable, gamified experience.

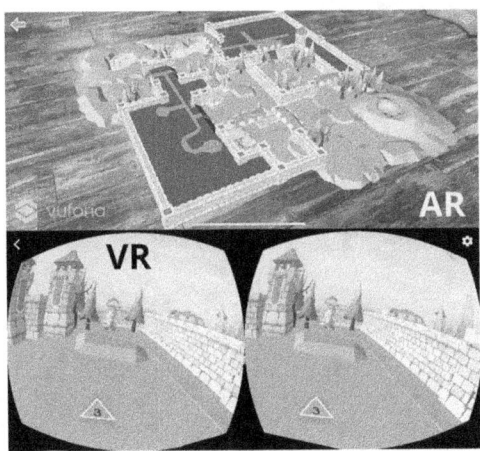

Figure 4.6. Scan the QR code and then the image to discover how Kai's Clan uses both AR and VR.

Adapting to changes is a necessary skill, and students are taught to be flexible from the very beginning of their educational journey. When students are given an opportunity to become problem solvers, the results are positive. They cleverly find solutions that some adults might not. Our students can adapt more easily because they've been conditioned to constantly adjust.

 ## Immersive Learning Challenge

Using both AR and VR tools, have your students app smash at least three apps to include created or scanned 3D objects and 360-degree images within a single project. Share your ideas on social media using #ARVRinEDU.

5 Personalized Devices

Device compatibility is one of the most common issues districts face when implementing immersive technology. The decision to make specific device purchases is often connected to lowest cost and ease of management. While budgets play a major role in determining purchases, the goal is to purchase devices that meet the needs of your students and curriculum while being compatible and functional in your district's technology infrastructure.

When determining the best devices for implementing immersive technology, there are a few key areas to address. I recommend you take the following steps before making a device purchase:

- Make sure goals and objectives for the technology are clearly identified.
- Consider how the devices you're considering can best reach the expected outcome.
- Consult the budget manager for assistance in identifying devices that work for current and future goals.
- Invite educator and student input to determine which device will be effective and receive maximum usage.

The budget your school or district is operating under will likely play a large role in any device purchase. However, making price the most important consideration is not the best approach. When placing cost as the first priority, the purchaser will inevitably filter results to view the cheapest options. Rather than identifying the best devices for your needs, the choices will be narrowed down to "getting the most bang for your buck," even if what you get isn't at all what you want or need.

A good way to approach a device purchase is by beginning with your intended goals. Identify which devices function best to achieve your expected outcomes. Create a list of needs and wants based on the purpose of the devices. The purchaser can then narrow down the search according to these criteria and determine a feasible quantity based on the budget.

Especially in this era of rapidly expanding choices for immersive tools, it's important to find the right device to match current needs as well as plans for upcoming changes. The best approach for spending designated funds is to have a short- and long-term device plan. Part of making long-term plans is doing your homework on upcoming changes and options in immersive technology. While the best resources are typically cross-platform, the compatible devices are generally newer and work with the latest features. Considering how quickly these devices are updated, the best option is typically selecting the technology that is most current, rather than purchasing an older version for a discount.

I've had numerous conversations with administrators about regrets when making certain technology purchases. They wish their current devices would function with more AR/VR tools. An important consideration when selecting the right device is the limitations of specific devices. For example, compatibility with specific AR/VR features can vary greatly on an iPad depending on the year, model, speed, and storage. As I've said before, it's important to do your homework!

Remote Learning

The demand for remote learning has grown considerably after the COVID-19 pandemic left many schools paralyzed. Stunned by the dramatic adjustments required, many U.S. schools were unprepared for distance learning. When districts finally figured out a way to connect virtually, they lacked the knowledge to truly engage students and provide student creation opportunities in a virtual environment. While many campuses were able to check the box for "teacher-student connections," most lacked the training to provide meaningful learning experiences in the new distanced format.

One of the substantial barriers many educational institutions faced when supporting distance learning was the lack of devices for students learning from home. The majority of U.S. schools have not fully transitioned to 1:1 devices, making it difficult to budget for such a massive purchase on short notice. In addition to devices, many U.S. students still do not have access to the internet. As schools scramble to meet these new demands, finding a device that can meet all your goals and objectives can be challenging. To help you in your decision making, the following section shares desirable features for immersive technology devices.

What to Look for in Immersive Technology Devices

Below is a list of device capabilities necessary for immersive technology to remain compatible with new and upcoming immersive applications.

AR (Mobile and Tablets)

ARKit and ARCore

One of the most significant upgrades to mobile AR has taken place in the past few years with the release of ARKit. Apple AR updates should have a minimum A12 chip to function best with current and upcoming features. The Android version of ARKit was initially referred to as ARCore, but is now known as Google Play Services for AR. While many Android devices now function with AR capabilities, select a 64-bit device to perform best with the latest apps. Some of the latest AR features include motion capture and occlusion. Capturing motion allows for tracking an individual and layering information on top, such as a skeleton layered on top of a person, moving with the individual. The occlusion feature layers 3D content in a set space to be in front of or behind real-world objects. Both of these features provide a more realistic AR experience.

3D Landscape Scanning versus Photogrammetry

3D landscape scanning is the next wave of the future as it uses location anchoring to immediately use latitude, longitude, and altitude. The new feature uses the device camera for depth sensing and can scan an area to capture a 3D map of your space. The name LIDAR stands for light detection and ranging. Essentially, LIDAR sends out a laser to measure precise measurements and details to map out the 3D terrain of a region.

An alternative to 3D landscape scanning, photogrammetry uses photos taken from various vantage points to rebuild a region by stitching those photos together into a 3D terrain. An example of photogrammetry is found in Google Earth, where the user can explore various locations and get a modest 3D experience based on the collected photos that Google Earth stitches together.

In most cases, LIDAR is going to provide more details of the space to provide the user the details necessary to "walk into" an immersive experience. The details are more than just images layered together, but millions of detected points of 3D objects in the space to accurately display and navigate around the site. The rumored Apple glasses are expected to include the new LIDAR technology as an immersive wearable device. Wearable technology has been anticipated for at least the past five years as Apple has ramped up mobile devices to function with ARKit. The release date has continued to be pushed, but there is no doubt that the technology will fit well in the current consumer market and open a huge potential in education.

High-End VR Headsets

6DoF for Positional Tracking

When the first wave of consumer VR headsets was released, the standard expectation was an upgraded Google Cardboard experience with a remote. The new standard for the most immersive experiences is six degrees of freedom (6DoF), which allows the user to navigate in their physical space while the headset tracks the movements. A student can now move forward, backward, left, and right, jump up, or squat down. Tracking these movements makes the experience much more realistic, and I've noticed a significant reduction in the nausea some users experience during VR use. With dual remotes and flexible movement, students can build, create, dissect, draw, play, and more. Having adequate space is an important consideration with devices that allow this level of freedom. If space is limited, having many devices running at the same time won't be possible.

Standalone Devices

Breaking free from cords and expensive computers is one of the most enticing reasons to purchase a VR headset. Many headsets are now completely standalone, making it much easier for the consumer to purchase these immersive products without onerous amounts of technical knowledge or a huge budget. I recommend standalone VR headsets for the classroom as they can eliminate the headaches of cords, additional training, and expensive computer purchases.

Management

Device management programs are an absolute must when introducing VR headsets into the classroom. Students will test the limits of the VR headsets, and most of the devices have open app marketplaces with non-educational or inappropriate content. While I'm a huge fan of Vader Immortal on the Oculus Quest, I don't want my students playing the VR game instead of studying ocean life. Management of these devices, especially with multiple devices in the classroom, is necessary, but still a work in progress. Before buying any device, confirm that your IT can support your students with a safe, immersive experience.

Established and Long-Standing Marketplace for Applications

I'm always skeptical when it comes to venturing into app marketplaces that are tied to a single device. When considering devices, the associated app marketplace should be established and compatible with other devices. Investment in apps can be quite costly, and without competition, variety, and compatibility on other devices, the risk for sustaining your immersive technology program is higher. Select devices that can access rich content but are not restricted to an app marketplace that may not be around very long.

Eye, Finger, and Body Tracking

Artificial intelligence (AI) capabilities are growing in demand and popularity in VR headsets. AI-enhanced features such as eye, finger, and body tracking allow users to interact with and control the experience in VR in a way that feels more authentic and requires a shorter learning curve than with remote control devices.

Cross-Platform Learning

Now more than ever, our educational system must be adaptable to meet our students where they are, regardless of location. With many districts scrambling to get a device in the hands of remote learners, we've learned that not all devices can provide the same opportunities. As districts face how to combine engagement during in-person or virtual learning with classroom content, the list of available applications shrink when limited by computers or laptops, especially with immersive technology.

The best opportunities for immersive learning are currently found in mobile devices. Although high-end AR and VR devices exist, they are typically less likely to be found in a classroom.

The most flexible and desirable AR/VR resources are those that are cross-platform. The most used immersive technology resources are those that work with computers, laptops, mobile devices, and high-end AR and VR headsets. These resources will be found mainly in something called WebXR.

WebXR

WebXR is a programming interface that delivers immersive experiences on the web. You may have already noticed some of these experiences when Google began adding animals in the search engine that can easily be seen in 3D and AR. Since that first release, Google has made more AR experiences available in your mobile browser—featuring dinosaurs and insects; planets, moons, and NASA objects; and bodily systems and other science models. As long as your device is AR enabled, you can use WebXR to explore immersive technology via the web without downloading an application. Try it out by searching for an animal or one of the things mentioned above in Google on your mobile device. Look for the button that says, "View in 3D" and see the object appear. To watch a video on how to explore Google AR, scan the QR code and view the image in Figure 5.1.

Figure 5.1. View a video on how to explore Google AR. Scan the QR code, and then keep this figure in view.

VR meeting spaces are another WebXR resource growing in popularity. Using sites like Hubs, students can connect and collaborate via high-end VR headsets, mobile devices, computers, and laptops by using the web browser. Not all VR meeting spaces allow users to access the space on multiple devices.

I believe WebXR is the future of many AR/VR experiences. The benefits of WebXR include speed, no need for storage, and compatibility across multiple operating systems, browsers, and devices without being tied to a specific app marketplace. Although WebXR is not yet as robust as other immersive technology applications, it does offer a great immersive experience.

Kit Ideas

There is a high level of interest in purchasing immersive kits for the classroom. Many technology companies recognized this interest and immediately jumped on the opportunity to sell high-priced kits with little flexibility or customization for students. Often, these sets were difficult to set up and stressful to troubleshoot. The concept of a kit seemed simple, but when placed in a district situation, it was not always worth the investment.

Considering this interest in kits, I've researched ways to make your own kits that are more affordable and practical for classroom use. I recommend fairly recent devices that function with many AR/VR resources. I typically recommend that districts purchase iPads for the most immersive options, but some districts prefer VR viewers to offer students 360-degree experiences and eliminate distractions. Table 5.1 shares some cost estimates and product recommendations to spark ideas. The costs are based on 2020 pricing and subject to change.

Table 5.1. Recommendations for AR/VR Kit (Pricing current as of 2020)

KIT COMPONENT	PRODUCT RECOMMENDATION	ESTIMATED COST
Devices	Apple iPod Touch (apple.com/ipod-touch)	$199 x 10 = **$1990**
Protective Cases		$19.99 x 10 = **$199.90**
Headsets	MERGE Headsets (shop.mergeedu.com/products/merge-vr-goggles-2)	$29.99 x 10 = **$299.90**
Charging Case	A variety are available on Amazon, including the Luxor Office Classroom Libraries 12 Outlet Wall/Desk Tablet Charging Box	**$178.78 each**
		TOTAL = $2668.58

Note that this kit is limited to ten devices. Considering most school network limitations, having every student on an AR/VR device at the same time isn't always possible, so stations would make the most sense for the majority of lessons. The charging case can be mobile or stationary, depending on your needs.

> ### Cleaning Supplies
>
> Keeping COVID-19 and other health regulations in mind, the best possible scenario would be to purchase the quantity needed to avoid passing devices from student to student. Whether or not this scenario is possible, you *must* include cleaning supplies in the budget when purchasing devices, especially when using them with viewers that contact students' noses, mouths, eyes, ears, hands, and hair.
>
> Cleaning products to consider:
>
> - Disinfectant wipes
> - Microfiber cloths
> - VR disposable mask pads
> - VR silicone cover face mask

Creating district-wide kits may require more research and a more detailed approach. An excellent example of immersive technology kits created for a district is from Kim Murphree, Educational Technology Trainer at Mansfield ISD in Texas. Her district was ready to integrate AR/VR into the curriculum but didn't have access to the right devices across the schools.

The district response to the kits was so overwhelmingly positive that, after receiving a grant, the curriculum and educational technology department purchased a second kit. The most important factors that led to success included training, promotion, and a strategic process that was perfected over time. While the kits specifically targeted a VR experience for the students, the flexibility of the devices provided the added benefit of AR experiences and creation. The Mansfield ISD team was able to find the right devices for the specific objectives and needs of their students. Now that Murphree has had a chance to go through the process, she recommends the following best practices when purchasing kits:

- Know your goal. Narrow your focus and concentrate on that.
- Innovate like a turtle. Start small, figure out your systems (what you need, what your resources are, and how you will implement), and slowly expand.
- Be innovative! Get creative, and get others involved!

The Mansfield ISD kit purchase is broken down in Table 5.2.

Table 5.2. The Mansfield ISD AR/VR Kit Purchase (Pricing current as of 2020)

VENDOR	PRODUCT	DESCRIPTION	PURPOSE	QTY	PRICE PER UNIT
MERGE	MERGE headsets	VR headset	View experiences in VR	35	$29.00 (- EDU Discount)
Apple	Apple iPod Touch (7th generation)	Mobile device	Devices	36	$199.99
Amazon	Router	NETGEAR R6700 Nighthawk AC1750 Dual Band Smart WiFi Router, Gigabit Ethernet (R6700)	Used to connect the devices to each other for Expeditions	1	$80.00
	Charging Block	Sabrent 10-Port Family-Sized Desktop Rapid Charger, Smart USB Ports with Auto Detect Technology, Black (AX-TPCS)	Charging blocks for devices	4	$29.00
	Small Totes	STERILITE 17511712 6-Quart Clearview Latch Storage Container with Plum Handles	Holds all student devices and charging cables	2	$7.00
	Large Tote	STERILITE 40 Gal./151 L Wheeled Industrial Tote	Holds all the things	1	$22.00
Dollar Tree	Pencil Case	Basic Multipurpose Utility Box	Holds teacher device	1	$1.00

Grant Possibilities

One of the biggest hesitations to embracing immersive technology in the classroom is the lack of funding to purchase devices that can support the latest resources. As Kim Murphree would say, "You miss 100 percent of the shots you don't take, so write the grant!"

If no appropriate devices are available in your district, consider submitting grant applications to seek funding for device purchases. Educational foundations, parent-teacher associations, private donors, Walmart, Target, and local companies are all good places to start. There are also state and national opportunities.

The massive list of current educational grants is extensive and exhausting to research. Try applying filters to specify location, subject, grade level, time limits, availability of awards, or how the grant money can be used. A wonderful resource with direct links to hundreds of grant opportunities is provided by MERGE EDU at mergeedu.com/edu-resources/funding. Don't forget to apply for training grants for the new devices!

Immersive Learning Challenge

Students can jump into a WebXR experience such as Hubs using multiple devices that are available in your classroom. Invite them to customize their own VR meeting spaces in Spoke to make the WebXR experience relevant for classmates. Share your experience on social media using #ARVRinEDU.

6 AR/VR in the Classroom: Personalized Experiences

In most classrooms we have a mix of students, some of whom need not just various alterations and adjustments to the same activities, but a completely different experience. Some students thrive with hands-on activities, while others prefer written or oral assignments. The beauty of AR/VR is that all these preferences can be included as you plan your lessons.

Personalized activities are often hindered in a remote learning environment. Many teachers struggle to get a single remote assignment delivered and graded, let alone provide different assignments for different types of learners. Evaluating a variety of activities may feel overwhelming, but it's time well spent. Consider creating a catalog of tools to supplement or replace activities that may constrain your students from getting a deeper understanding of the concepts.

Following are some suggestions for personalized activities using AR/VR tools.

Scavenger Hunts with Scavengar EDU

As mentioned before, Scavengar provides a simple platform for classrooms to create and participate in scavenger hunts. Scavenger hunts have always captured our students' attention, and playing in AR makes them even more enticing. Scavengar EDU is a new platform specifically designed for the classroom. Educators can share the hunts by link, and students can join in and play. Scavengar collects and displays data regarding how quickly the hunt was completed, the correct responses (determined by points), and responses via GIFs, text, and images. The hunts are protected in the Scavengar EDU app; they aren't visible to the public as they were in the basic app. Stay tuned: more options are coming soon to make sharing scavenger hunts effortless and more engaging, and to provide better hunt management functionality.

The new education version of Scavengar allows teachers and students to upload 3D content to the hunt. The teaching aids that we often can't have in our classroom are now possible in this app using digital, 3D objects. Students can create artifacts from history and build a world hunt to find the items. They can do this in their classroom or at home! Use 3D objects to collect characters from a story or to identify the different parts of a cell. If you haven't created your own 3D objects, many items may be downloaded in the USDZ format from Sketchfab or USDZshare.com.

In addition to exploring the objects, students can respond to questions about the object via multiple-choice answers. The teacher can allow GIF responses that are collected and visible to all those participating in the hunt. Scavengar EDU also has integrated machine learning as students must find specific items or dominant colors in the hunt by capturing a picture of the object. Some of these items include animals, nature items, fruit, transportation objects, furniture, and other common items. The teacher might ask the student to capture a photo with a specific dominant color. If the student succeeds in capturing a photo with the color requested, they will earn the points for a correct answer. Receiving this type of feedback in a scavenger hunt app is not common, especially in AR, making this app stand out.

The beauty of Scavengar is the ability to participate in the hunt from anywhere. While the hunts can be location-based, the option of setting up the hunt in your own space is a great way to get your students up and moving from anywhere. This is especially true for our remote learners who can't scan pages or go to a specific location to identify the next clue. In this situation the hunt will identify the space using the camera, and then place the hunt within those boundaries.

> ### Join a Scavenger Hunt!
>
> Download the app using the QR code and explore Scavengar EDU while participating in my AR scavenger hunt! In the app, select the settings button in the top left, and then "Open Hunt via Link" and type in vy6BK712fab
>
>

Breakouts Using CoSpaces

There are many options in the CoSpaces platform, from learning code to creating AR scenes to building VR experiences using 360-degree images. Students have found many ways to creatively build in this platform, including creating scavenger hunts, games, murder mystery scenes, Where's Waldo scenes, vacation building scenes, mazes, theme parks, and egg hunts. Since the product is so versatile, students have found ways to make it work for any grade level, subject, and lesson.

Another creative way to use CoSpaces is by building an escape room, often referred to in education as a breakout. After I explored a few breakouts designed by students in CoSpaces, it became clear that they completed these projects by overcoming many obstacles and learning new coding skills. Moving from space to space, I collected keys and remotes to open doors and turn on media. After visiting the breakout in a 360-degree VR scene on my computer, I then explored the breakout in my living room by experiencing it in AR. I walked from room to room while capturing and opening items by tapping on my mobile device. The experience was incredible, both in VR and AR.

Figure 6.1. Challenge your breakout abilities in this interactive CoSpace created by Sebastianeisele. Scan the QR code or go to bit.ly/cospaceschallenge to join the breakout.

Creating breakouts in AR/VR with CoSpaces is similar to the concept of creating physical breakouts in the classroom. The content in the breakout is the most difficult and vital part as it requires planning. After the content is collected and planned, students can begin building the space in CoSpaces. Using CoBlocks, students can transform, add responses, create events, include conditions, and insert controls, logic, and variables on the library items in the space. Advanced students can use the physics operations to modify objects in the scene.

A great edtech friend, Morgan Lucas, has created lessons during which her middle school students create breakout experiences using CoSpaces. Her students have been able to make incredible breakouts, mainly learning by trial and error. Some of her students work in groups to create the spaces, while others work independently. Some students even build the spaces to include audio and video recording, which creates realistic interactions.

The creative work of the students is off the charts and the diligence required by the students is immediately met with celebration and praise by Lucas. One of her students created a breakout space that required the user to make it through the entire house without waking up the sleeping man on the couch. Waking the man up causes you to instantly be pulled back to the beginning of the breakout. Although it took me several tries, I was finally successful in getting through the house.

Science Labs

The subject of science has always surpassed other subjects in the number of immersive technology experiences possible. The popularity of science experiences may be due to science lessons' tendencies towards hands-on experiments and content, which become easy visuals to explore in immersive technology. AR/VR apps offer endless lab experiments, and finding the perfect classroom option is easier than most think.

The use of immersive dissection labs has grown in popularity for several reasons. Probably the most obvious reason for moving to AR/VR options is funding limitations. Schools are finding it ever more difficult to budget for dissection specimens. Another rationale for moving to AR/VR options is the demand for more humane approaches to research and learning. While the quality of the knowledge acquired by the real dissection versus the virtual dissection is debatable, I find the virtual experiences to be quite valuable for my students.

THE IMMERSIVE CLASSROOM

Some immersive science lab apps require high-end VR headsets, while others are possible on mobile devices. The key to a great virtual experience is deciding what important objectives you plan to cover and determining if your devices are compatible with the available apps. When using many VR headsets, the labs require the use of two remotes and place the experiments in a dynamic laboratory space. It's often possible to have a virtual lab space with the instructor and students joining in the space at the same time. One platform that has been used for such experiences is Engage, a virtual meeting space used by schools, businesses, and others.

VictoryXR

One company that uses Engage to provide interactive science labs is VictoryXR. Using NGSS, TEKS, and CPALMS standards, VictoryXR has created a platform of middle school and high school immersive science content, mainly for high-end VR headsets. I've joined the VictoryXR campus in Engage for a live demo that included a lesson presented by a teacher and delivered to students. The VictoryXR campus provides the virtual space, more than three thousand correlating 3D objects, and more than one hundred virtual field trips.

In addition to the VictoryXR campus, the company has invested in other immersive experiences including augmented reality. Through the use of books, cards, and even a plastic torso called Victor, the learning comes to life in AR as students examine science concepts such as astronomy, physics, and life science. The AR

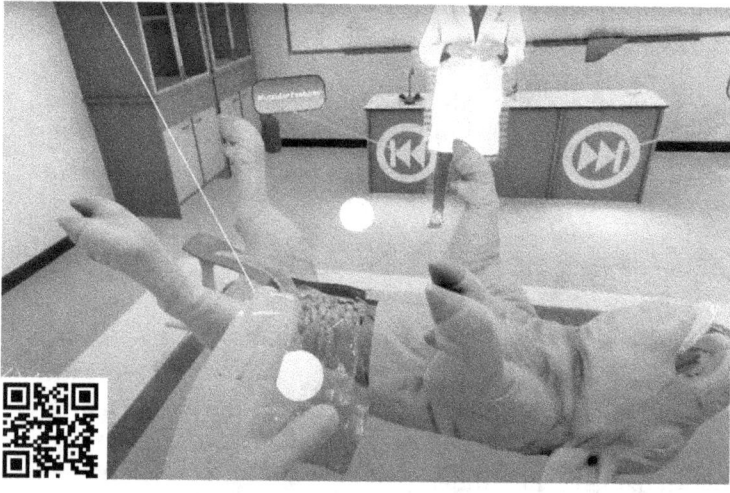

Figure 6.2. VictoryXR pig dissection. Learn more by scanning this figure using the Arloopa app available at arloopa.com or the QR code.

experiences work with a mobile device and scan the trigger images (the cards, book, and plastic torso) to display the content on top.

My first encounter with VictoryXR was dissecting a pig in virtual reality. Using dual remotes, I was able to dissect and inspect the pig's organs while being guided by an award-winning science teacher Wendy Martin, who was presented as a holographic assistant. The dissection used realistic tools and the experience for me was intense, even though I was fully aware that I was performing the task in virtual reality. For anyone who has performed a dissection in real life, the best part about doing the dissection in VR was the lack of that formaldehyde smell!

MEL Science

For a more independent VR lab experience, students can explore MEL Chemistry. The MEL Chemistry app places the student in the center of a high-tech laboratory to discover classroom content using a VR headset or in a 3D environment on mobile devices. Here students will study some of the most difficult concepts in chemistry in a visually appealing, interactive virtual environment using a mobile device. MEL Science is most known for taking complex concepts and breaking them down to the molecular level. Using VR, the app demonstrates the connections between the macro and micro worlds, making the invisible, visible.

In the VR lab, students have the option to connect to an online teacher to run the lessons from a single device. Students will be guided by the teacher in the lesson using the IP address of that teacher's device. Especially in a remote learning environment, it is essential that students can explore while being guided by an educator who can pause the screen and explain concepts or answer questions. There is a subscription fee for educators who use this functionality.

Human Anatomy Atlas by Visible Body

The Atlas AR app by Visible Body places an AR human cadaver in your classroom with a full anatomy contained inside. Students may explore the various body systems and dissect layer by layer.

I took my son to our chiropractor, Dr. Charles Dixon, because he was having back and neck pain. Dr. Dixon recommended acupuncture after observing and evaluating my son's situation. My curiosity got the best of me, and I began chatting with Dr. Dixon about the procedure.

As the chiropractor began explaining his process, I was having a hard time following which muscles he was referring to, and why he would need to move between

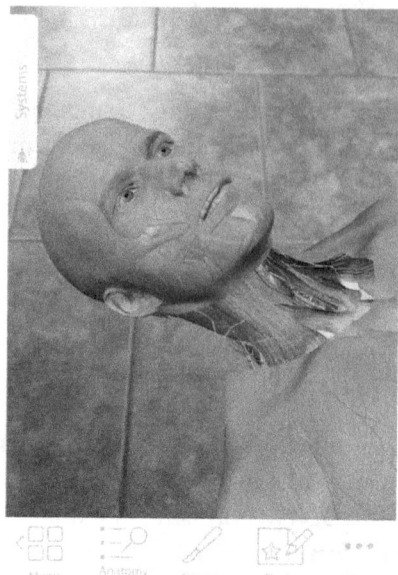

Figure 6.3. View a video of the Atlas AR app by scanning this figure in the Arloopa app.

multiple muscles to get to the specific ones that were causing my son pain. He decided to explain to me what muscles he was targeting by walking me to a poster hanging on the wall that showed the human neck and back muscles. I became even more confused about the complexity of the layered muscles. I asked if it was ok to show him the Atlas AR app and allow him to describe the process on a 3D human cadaver on the office floor.

The realistic human body shown in AR was exactly what I needed to finally understand what he was trying to explain. The app allows you to dissect each part of the human body, one tap at a time. Dr. Dixon began tapping the neck and back muscles one at a time as he worked down little by little to finally show me the muscles he was targeting with acupuncture. I was blown away with how many muscles he had to get through in order to reach the problematic muscles. There is no way that a 2D picture could deliver the same learning experience as I received from the Atlas AR app. I needed that type of learning experience to fully grasp the concept, and I can imagine many of our students can relate.

A word of caution about this particular app: it features the full anatomy of the human body and may not be appropriate for some age groups.

MERGE Explorer Frog Dissection

Another mobile dissection app is found in MERGE Explorer. The specific card for frog dissection is called A Frog's Life and covers each stage of the frog life cycle, starting at eggs and concluding with dissection of the adult frog. The mobile app includes a variety of other science simulations, perfect for classroom labs.

After opening the MERGE Explorer app, scroll down and select the A Frog's Life card. As with every card, the content is available even before you explore the AR experience. Students will explore the life cycle of the frog in the first activity. The play button will open your camera to find the MERGE Cube. When the MERGE Cube appears, the app will place the frog eggs inside the cube. Make the experience larger or smaller by swiping up or down on the screen with one finger. Select the Next button at the bottom of the screen to explore each cycle. Watch the embryo, tadpole, froglet, and adult frog transition from stage to stage within the cube (see Figure 6.4).

The next activity is focused on the anatomy of the frog as compared to a similar layout of the human anatomy. This humane process is often more appealing for students and teachers, and it is especially valuable in a remote environment. The

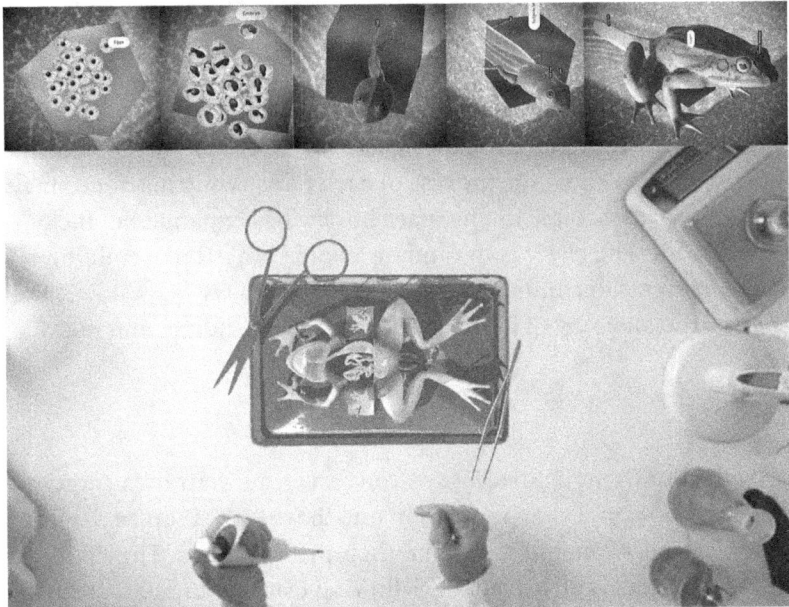

Figure 6.4. A Frog's Life experience in the MERGE Explorer app allows users to dissect a virtual frog using a MEREG Cube. See the dissection by scanning the QR code (or going to mywebar.com/pi/4474) and then viewing the image. Tap the overlay to see it come to life.

dissection process shows the liver, heart, lungs, and stomach. The learner separates each organ using the slider at the bottom of the page, then taps an organ to label it. To get a larger view, simply swipe up on the screen.

The final step for this card is completing the activity quiz. The quiz completion confirmation and lesson resources are found on the MERGE dashboard. The quiz can only be completed when all the answers are correct, and each grade level quiz targets the appropriate NGSS standards. MERGE provides activity plans for grades K-2, 3-5, and 6-8 on every topic card in the MERGE Explorer app.

> **Try the MERGE Cube before buying one!**
>
> If you don't have a MERGE Cube yet but are curious to see the functionality, download a printable cube to view the experience at arvrinedu.com/post/merge-cube-printable.

Interactive Presentations with JigSpace

The JigSpace app is the first of its kind to essentially show how things work in augmented reality. From the inside of a battery to a jet engine, JigSpace delivers an immersive "un-slideshow" of content. The experiences are delivered in 3D presentations that transition "slides" to show the process of each part. While machines may not seem relevant to most classrooms, the JigSpace library has expanded to include science and history content. The classroom can now explore an AR presentation on the human ear, heart stents, tectonic plates, the NASA Curiosity Mars Rover, Da Vinci's *Scythed Chariot*, the anatomy of a trebuchet, the D-Day landing, and many other experiences.

Jig Workshop

Don't feel limited by the library in JigSpace. Now you can create your own content using the free Jig Workshop app. Using more than one thousand 3D objects in the Jig Workshop library, teachers can add items into their presentations. The option to upload your own 3D objects is also available, allowing teachers to build customized AR presentations for all content and grade levels. Additionally, imagine your students building their presentations in Jig Workshop rather than submitting work in Google Slides.

This immersive way of presenting content is much more relevant and realistic for displaying knowledge and understanding. Simply sharing a link allows students to independently explore your lesson. Another option allows the teacher to control each step, with students' screens displaying only the slide that the teacher is showing. The microphone is available for educators and students to collaborate in real time while the AR presentation is taking place.

Jig Workshop provides an immersive and practical delivery of content for remote learning. Whether your students join your session on their own or as a whole class, they can personalize the learning by walking around and exploring the 3D content from any view they prefer. As an added bonus, JigSpace and Jig Workshop include AR people occlusion, making the experience more realistic as it layers objects in front of and behind the people standing in the scene.

> **See an example of Jig Workshop in action!**
>
> Download the Jig Workshop app and then scan the QR code (or go to bit.ly/examplejigspace) to view my example on your mobile device.

Create Your Own Augmented Reality

For years following the failure of HP Reveal (formerly Aurasma), I've received countless requests for tools to create augmented reality. Today there are new resources for building amazing content that can be made effective and practical for the classroom. Below are the best of these AR creation resources.

Arloopa Studio

Arloopa Studio is an online creation platform to build immersive experiences. The studio is currently in beta mode but still has quite a bit to offer. The simple creation process begins with three options: marker-based (using a trigger image), marker-less (placed in your space), and location-based experiences. Each of these options allows the user to add AR using 3D objects or video content.

Sketchfab and Unity integrations are upcoming features, but in the meantime you can connect most objects in Google Poly. Arloopa also allows the user to upload videos or 3D GLB files to use in the experience, or to link a YouTube video in the scene. The web-based platform and flexibility in this product make it a great fit for classrooms.

THE IMMERSIVE CLASSROOM

EyeJack

The free EyeJack app easily makes simple video overlays on top of an image. The user-generated feed is not classroom appropriate at times, so I'd recommend a product like this for higher education or adult professional development. Additionally, the application must be installed on a computer, making it difficult for classrooms that have Chromebooks. The EyeJack team is working on a classroom product that would eliminate the feed in the future.

Assemblr Studio

Similar to EyeJack, the Assemblr Studio app must be installed on a computer. The functionality of Assemblr is much more elaborate—students can load more than video content on top of an image. The application has a vast 3D library of educational content that will suit many lessons in various grades and subjects. Many of the objects are animated, making the experiences more realistic.

The free version of Assemblr layers items on top of a QR code, rather than layering on top of an image. Students can upload 3D content in Assemblr, but the storage size is extremely small. A beneficial feature in Assemblr allows you to add multiple scenes, making it possible to create an entire story on top of a single QR code.

Figure 6.6. View an AR scene of animated zoo animals created in the Assemblr Studio application. Open the Assemblr app and scan the QR code to view.

MyWebAR.com

MyWebAR.com is by far my favorite AR creation tool. In contrast to the other tools mentioned above, MyWebAR.com doesn't require an app to populate the experience; rather it uses the browser (WebXR) on the device to populate the augmented reality. I anticipate that the new app clips will be a big part of web-based AR to make the transition to content much faster and easier. MyWebAR.com was created by the incredible DEVAR team, already producing vast amounts of educational content such as books, cards, toys, games, shirts, and more.

The visual web editor provides everything you need to create AR for your classroom. Students can add AR on images, the floor, or a QR code. The visual editor connects many other 3D objects to add into the space, and the user can customize where all the items should go and how they should react in the scene. Many file formats are accepted for video and 3D content uploads. With over one thousand 3D objects available in the library, classrooms can create many customizable experiences.

Limited by Location? 360-Degree Learning Can Help

It's no surprise that classrooms find a way to bring immersive, personalized activities into their lessons, even when the classroom device is limited. Some resources work great in the browser and Google's Tour Creator is a perfect match for our Chromebook campuses. One of the most knowledgeable people I know about all things Google is Debra Atchison. She has trained across the world using Google tools and other emerging technologies with administrators, teachers, and students, allowing them to get the most benefit from their classroom devices.

Atchison has worked with schools that have made the switch to Chromebooks and are looking for options to build VR content. She recommends using the free, web-based Tour Creator option that can use Google 360 images and their own content. According to Atchison, many elementary classrooms already use Google Expeditions as an entry point for immersive technology, so this creates a perfect transition to the creation platform of Tour Creator. She reminds Google Suite Administrators that they must turn on Tour Creator in the admin console under "other apps" for teachers and students to access the site.

One of the best educational examples Atchison witnessed in Tour Creator was made by classroom teacher Tammy Whitaker of Wills Point ISD in Texas. Her students were limited by their exposure to various developed environments. Whitaker created a tour to support her students in understanding the differences between urban, suburban, and rural areas. The immersive experience brought students from New York to Dallas to Terrell to Forney and back to their small town. The students responded to the virtual tour with pure joy as they made immediate and lasting connections to the content.

> Check out a VR tour created by Tammy Whitaker in Tour Creator by scanning the QR code or going to bit.ly/whitakertour. When Tour Creator is finally closed, view the tour at bit.ly/tourtammy.

Google gave the news that Tour Creator was shutting down in June of 2021 due to low usage. While Tour Creator is a flexible resource across many devices, it's also served as a perfect resource for remote learning. As an alternative, another web-based tour creation option besides RoundMe is available. The Klapty website offers many of the same features of Tour Creator and more, but similar to RoundMe, lacks the option to include 360 images from Google Maps. The Klapty sharing feature is more robust than Tour Creator and the embed code is perfect for classrooms to include on school websites.

Many of our classrooms have video chats for our students and indeed, Zoom and other videoconferencing tools have become the norm since the COVID-19 pandemic began. By including virtual tours in these meetings, you can transport students outside of the routine and into incredible, virtual learning experiences. Simply sharing a link to a tour in a video chat can bring students on a learning journey to locations around the world. Better yet, ask students to build a virtual tour on historical landmarks, landforms, spatial forms of buildings (geometry), museums, or college campuses and ask them to share their tours with others in the class.

 ## Immersive Learning Challenge

Using one of the AR creation tools from this chapter, ask students to build an experience using 3D objects they've designed or library items within the platform. Encourage them to add their own details to the immersive experience. Share the link to the AR project on social media using #ARVRinEDU.

AR/VR in the Classroom: Immersive Activities to Inspire Learning

One of the most common goals for immersive technology is creating in students an incentive to learn. Not only do AR/VR experiences interest our students, they can also provide them with the enthusiasm to want to learn.

I often share my resources with my extended family, especially when I learn of new tools or get new devices. My two nephews, Jayden and Jace, have taken a special interest in exploring the latest AR/VR tools. Being just as enthusiastic as I am about this new technology, they're willing to help me figure out how everything works. At the start of the COVID-19 pandemic, I introduced them to CoSpaces after recognizing their passion for storytelling.

A few days after adding them to my CoSpaces class, I received a message to check out the spaces they had created. I was amazed at how much time they spent on their spaces and the strategy they used to tell a story. As they explained the purpose of each space, they shared with me the resources they had used when they were limited to only the 3D library items. I then shared ways to find other 3D items through the search, but we couldn't find the perfect match.

Another tool came to mind when they began creating new objects by combining the simple shapes available in the library. I recommended creating 3D objects using Tinkercad and importing those objects into CoSpaces. They were no longer limited by the library items but now had the opportunity to build exactly what they wanted. In the past few months, they continued building new spaces; they love it. They may not realize that creating 3D objects is a foundational skill that can become a future career, because all they focus on is the enjoyment of playing in CoSpaces.

Understanding our students' interests is just the beginning. Important areas to consider when making recommendations are:

- curriculum objectives
- access to specific devices and adequate internet
- attention span
- areas of struggle and strength
- collaboration opportunities and potential limitations
- access to support and guidance
- the next project using new skills

When students are learning because they enjoy it, not only do they retain more information, they go well beyond the basics of completing the assignment. I've never heard of students complaining about exploring or creating immersive projects. If we can maximize the benefits of AR/VR to uncover a passion for learning, we may see growth and achievement like we've never seen before. This chapter shares ways to inspire your individual students using immersive technology.

Writing and Literacy Tools

Storytelling with Face Replaced

AR face filters have been around for a while, with many social media companies building this functionality into their platform. While using a filter created by a developer may be fun, having the option to create your own AR face filter is an educational game changer. In Chapter 4, I shared the benefit of using Face Replaced when app smashing. The Face Replaced app allows users to create their own face filters; it uses the depth sensors in the mobile camera to scan a face and layers it on top of your own face. In addition to scanning a face, the user can load images and specify the facial structure to properly layer on another user's face.

The Face Replaced app can inspire students to become different characters and tell their stories. Students can create bibliographies of historical figures, tell the story of a character in a book, deliver a speech with famous quotes, or make predictions about famous people in the future. There are numerous ways for the student to be inspired to tell a story, and the Face Replaced app is simple, yet fun.

Figure 7.1. Be inspired to create your own stories using Face Replaced.

Inspire Writing with DrawmaticAR

One of my greatest academic struggles—one that continues to follow me—is writing. I didn't do much reading while in school and that naturally affected my writing skills. My lack of confidence when writing makes me less enthusiastic to write and instead, I am easily distracted.

For those students who may also have a negative attitude towards writing, there is an immersive technology tool that can help to create enthusiasm around the task. The DrawmaticAR app uses artificial intelligence to identify written words on a special worksheet, and then layers the matching 3D objects on the worksheet. Students will be amazed to see their written sentences come alive in AR on the worksheet. Even the most resistant writers will want to participate in this fun lesson, and as a bonus, the app gives immediate feedback on the readability and spelling of each student's work.

The DrawmaticAR.com website offers lesson plans, a free download of the special worksheet, and a library of 3D objects. A new update includes the option to have up to six languages translated and spoken on the highlighted nouns in the written sentences. The AR app can be found in the Apple VPP (Volume Purchase Program) to support multiple devices.

Inspire Literacy with DisruptED

Our younger learners typically don't get to use as many immersive technology resources as our older learners, but that's starting to change. The disruptED app

Figure 7.2. Bee Safe book with interactive content. Scan this image to see the page come to life using the disruptED app. Select the BEE SAFE book and then view in AR.

delivers immersive technology using the books they publish on the topics of letters, shapes, and opposites. While many AR/VR companies create good experiences, they rarely offer supporting resources for effective learning. DisruptED creates great experiences, activities, and lessons to provide the full curriculum on these topics for our younger learners.

The enthusiasm students show in response to the book content supported with AR/VR is exciting, especially when used as early intervention. The short AR/VR activities provide enough insight for students to make lasting connections with the concepts, and the activity book reinforces the new content for long term retention. The kit includes the books, a VR headset, activity books, and teacher guides.

A new book called *Bee Safe* is available to download for free (Figure 7.2). The book comes with a corresponding activity book and teacher lesson plans to begin using with students immediately. The content is focused on good hygiene, which is especially important for our little ones who are learning how to avoid spreading germs. The book also reassures our students that we don't have to "bee afraid." In addition to classroom content, a matching face mask and stickers are included in the kit.

Inspire Reading with Wonderscope

My oldest daughter Hannah has always been skilled in language arts. She beautifully articulates her thoughts, and I've always admired her strength in this area, because I'm completely on the other side. As a struggling reader, I would have rather gone to the principal's office than read in front of my peers. I recall once in a new middle school being asked to read a passage in a book, and when I got to the abbreviation "etc." I read each letter instead of reading the Latin word "et cetera." The class roared in laughter. Imagine how many other students feel that same embarrassment every time they're required to read in front of a group.

The Wonderscope app is intended to build confidence among young readers by enticing them to read the text in order to advance the AR story. The app scans the floor to identify where to place the story, and characters and story props appear all around the student.

Students must speak the commands at the bottom of the screen to move the story forward. This approach gives the reader the feeling that they are the center of the story and builds their confidence as the narrative continues. Every part of the Wonderscope app is targeted for interaction and engagement. Each story brings its own interesting challenges and keeps the reader engaged.

Immersive STEAM Activities

Inspire Coding Skills with Rox's Secret Code

A foundational skill for our students is an understanding and working knowledge of coding. I personally have little knowledge of coding, so I can understand why so many educators are hesitant to include this skill in their lessons. However, many coding programs today make it easy for anybody to begin and support quick growth.

Rox's Secret Code is perfect for students of all ages to learn the foundational concepts of coding. The beginning activities are simple, but they quickly become more and more difficult to challenge the user's problem-solving skills. The fun AR coding games begin with the customization of a robot and then move into performing tasks as the robot. The app has an accompanying customizable hardcover book in which you can modify the main character's appearance and name to match a particular student.

Maker Meets Immersive Technology with MEL Kids

MEL Kids identifies the maker in all of us, and the desire to play and create. Each kit includes a graphic novel and supplies for a project that the students will complete. The characters in the comic find themselves in need of help from your students; students will need to follow the instructions to build a functioning device.

The stories are full of imagery to captivate our students, but the building combined with the book makes this product stand out from the rest. Students will need to successfully complete the educational model to solve the problem and when they're done, they continue to play with their creation as they understand science concepts on a deeper level.

One of the maker kits includes a graphic novel about hydraulic lifts. To build the items, I asked my children, niece, nephews, and older brother to join me. Our initial thought was skipping the book altogether and moving right into the making. We soon realized that we needed to understand the story to know how to make the device. Having no knowledge or understanding of the concept myself, I was blown away with how much we learned in a short amount of time by building the device from scratch.

After the hydraulic lift was assembled, we began exploring what it could and couldn't lift. We first tested my niece Chelsea's Barbie dolls and found that air in the hydraulics system worked fine, but when we tried to add our full coffee cup on the lift, it wouldn't work. We found that adding water in the hydraulics system strengthened the lifting power. The conversation then moved to hydraulic fluid and its benefits as opposed to water. The process was fun and engaging for everyone, from the youngest child (seven years old) to the oldest adult (forty-five years old).

Inspire Creativity with Stickman AR and TokoToko

The Stickman AR app is one of a kind in offering imaginative play. Students can rescue friends trapped in the AR mystery story. The app requires the students to draw (on the mobile device) various characters and props to successfully win the game. The drawings on the device become part of the AR story and support the student to solve each problem they face.

The TokoToko app is similar to the Stickman AR app, but the story is geared toward older students. The interactions are spread out more than in Stickman AR and require more attention to the story. The story captures drawings on paper and layers them in the scene. Each character is full of personality, and students can personalize them by including their own artwork. Students will love interacting with these creative story puzzles, especially if they enjoy art.

Tools to Foster Problem Solving and Collaboration Skills

Problem Solving with Metaverse

As mentioned in Chapter 4, the Metaverse app is extremely versatile because it offers a huge amount of options for the user to create experiences. While the functionality is massive, the difficulty is also increased, because it requires the user to problem solve in certain instances. The storyboard can become very complicated when adding many cards. Students will need to use problem-solving strategies to overcome errors as they may not connect to the cards or the transition isn't set up properly.

Rachelle Dene Poth's class offered a perfect example of problem solving using Metaverse. She encouraged her students to get support from one another as they built their storyboards. Her students were successful in creating Metaverse experiences because when they were presented with challenges, they worked together and problem solved to find the solutions. Poth's classroom was able to embrace the most innovative technologies because she empowered her students to solve problems.

VR Escape Rooms

I recently hosted a VR escape room with a few #ARVRinEDU educator friends. The VR game I chose, Mr. Crumb's School for Disobedient Pets, required players to use an Oculus Quest; the number of participants was limited to four. We each role played as a pet in a virtual lab. I was Husky the dog, Caitlin Krause was Fancy Feast the cat, Elena Chopyak was Thumper the bunny, and Steve Isaacs was Tiny the hamster. Our objective was to infiltrate Mr. Crumb's school as new recruits and free the pets trapped there by solving a series of challenges that allowed us to move from room to room.

We each joined in from home through our Oculus Quests. The game has two characters who act as guides to provide support during any problems or dilemmas. The characters made the game more fun by keeping us laughing and moving forward. We had a solid group of players, so we successfully completed the task.

As a group, we all felt that this adventure surpassed our expectations and was well planned and coordinated. Although we couldn't see a direct connection to the classroom, we did see value for similar experiences tied to the curriculum, and especially for team-building activities. We played this escape room a few months into the COVID-19 pandemic, and one thing we all appreciated was feeling the deeper social connections made possible by this technology.

THE IMMERSIVE CLASSROOM

Figure 7.3. The VR Escape Room Experience in Mr. Crumb's School for Disobedient Pets. Watch the recap from our adventure at mywebar.com/pi/4499 on a mobile device.

Mindlabs

Create a digital circuit board playground as your students discover electricity. The Mindlabs app immerses your students in a story presented and supported by Atom, the robot. Students will join the challenges as they learn bit by bit the basics of circuits. Each challenge gets more difficult and requires problem solving to successfully stop the evil Dr. Stonebreaker. The Mindlabs app requires accompanying playing cards that deliver the AR play. The cards' subjects include batteries, light bulbs, fans, switches, and more.

As an added bonus, the updated Mindlabs app supports a creative play space where students can build and explore separate from the challenges. The students can build independently or work in groups of up to four at a time. This multiplayer collaboration is ideal for remote learning, because students can join from home or school, regardless of the location.

Figure 7.4. Download the Mindlabs app and select a challenge to get started. Scan the image to begin the experience. Find the remaining cards at exploremindlabs.com.

Health and Physical Education Tools

Apple Watch

Getting personalized and prescriptive activities can begin by collecting important health information. The Apple Watch collects information about our health including tracking high and low heart rate, irregular heart rhythms, blood oxygen levels, exercise, sleep trends, and more. The apps that work with the Apple Watch can send information to other devices and display that information in augmented and virtual reality. We will soon see more such integration in our wearables, especially as we approach the release of AR glasses.

Insight Heart

The Insight Heart app by Animares is an incredible tool that gives you a new perspective on your health. The AR app displays a heart outside of the body and shows how it responds to certain levels of exercise and stress. The visual encounter with the heart is somewhat surreal; as you walk around the heart, if you get close enough, you can feel the heart beating in your hand through haptic feedback on your mobile device.

In the app, students can explore and learn about different heart conditions such as myocardial infarction, arterial hypertension, and atrial fibrillation. Using an Apple Watch, students can download the Insight Heart app and track their own heart rates. When the app is opened on the Apple Watch, the heart view on the mobile device will visually show a small heart beating at the same rate as the student's. The app also offers a multi-user option to invite others to explore the AR heart together. The other users must be on the same network to join.

> Keep an eye out for the latest apps by Animares: Insight Lungs, Insight Virus, and Insight Bone. The body tracking in the Insight Bone app is truly remarkable and relevant for our students to bridge learning connections.

Supernatural

Another immersive technology integration with the Apple Watch is found in VR using the Oculus Quest. The Supernatural app is a new way to experience exercise and fitness. The app brings popular music, exercise, and a virtual fitness instructor into your home to support your exercise experience.

While using the Apple Watch with the app, your health data is tracked during the exercise and immediately following the activity, the user is able to see all the statistics from the exercise. Evaluating those analytics are important to determine the next selected activity. The analytics also provide encouragement as the user sees growth over time.

It's important to note that due to possibly inappropriate music, I wouldn't recommend using this app in a K–12 situation. I do recommend potentially using it in higher education. I'm sharing this tool because it's a new wave of exercise options that will be more popular in time. Another factor for this particular app is the potentially costly monthly or annual subscription fee to access the exercises.

Figure 7.5. Watch the integration of my Apple Watch with the Insight Heart app by opening the EyeJack app and scanning the QR code.

VR Exercise

Another exercise tracker connected to the Apple Watch is the VR Exercise app. The app collects information from various exercise apps in VR to determine how many calories are burned based on the specific exercise and its intensity. The app doesn't require specific tools like Supernatural, so the freedom to connect exercise data from any application is most beneficial. The VR Exercise app works with other wearables in addition to the Apple Watch.

Virtuali-Tee

Several years ago, a Kickstarter campaign with Curiscope began for the Virtuali-Tee shirt. The shirt has an image similar to a QR code that is scanned by the app to display an AR layer of the different body systems.

An update was released to track the heart rate of the user by shining a light from the camera onto the index finger. Once the app detects the heart rate, the beating heart image adjusts to match the heart rate of the person wearing the shirt. The update was a huge step for the classroom as there are few wearables used in education and the app and shirt combo is more practical and cost-effective than purchasing many smartwatches.

> The Curiscope team recently released a new science app with correlating posters called Curiscope Multiverse. Imagine the universe bursting through your classroom walls as your students explore interactive posters detailing the planets and solar system!

Immersive Learning Challenge

Invite students to choose a skill or content area that they want to work on and try using one of the tools from this chapter to explore it further. Ask, how did the immersive experience affect your learning? Share your thoughts on social media using #ARVRinEDU.

8 Personalized Experiences for All Students

With so many AR/VR resources coming out all the time, it's easy to get lost in the sea of immersive technology. I know the feeling. A new tool does something amazing, so you incorporate it into your next lesson—you know your students will enjoy the experience—stretching its connection to the content to make it work. Getting excited about immersive technology is understandable, but when there are so many options for using AR/VR, you don't need to force a square peg into a round hole.

When approaching any technology, we must identify and prioritize our goals. It's important to determine the best approach for our students and identify any possible limitations with delivering the content. We must consider first what our students need to know and master, placing their individual needs in line with our goals. The use of immersive technology has the potential to override typical classroom limitations, making the selection of the right tools for the right students that much more important.

Special consideration must also be provided to our students with disabilities. I shared the story of Trace in Chapter 2 and how he required a different technology than other children might when using VR. If I had placed the latest and greatest headset on Trace, he would have been extremely limited in his interactions and most likely, he would have asked to get out of the headset because it required too much mobility. His request to engage in VR must be met with the right tools for his particular needs.

Targeted Technology

Most immersive technology resources are designed for the general public and do not take individual needs into consideration. Rarely do we see AR/VR designed for targeted groups, likely because the risk of losing money is too high for companies if they eliminate their larger audience. However, targeted AR/VR apps do exist. When I share immersive technology, I tend to focus on ways to make the tools available for all, but sometimes, targeted resources better address individual needs. The following are examples of immersive technology tools for specific audiences and needs.

NarratorAR (Dyslexia)

When I first learned about the NarratorAR app from Debra Atchison (whose work with Google Tour Creator was shared in Chapter 6), I understood it as an introduction to letters. After exploring the app further, I noticed an incredible essential skill for letter and number formation was the spotlight. The main goal of NarratorAR is to motivate students to want to write letters and numbers by using AR. However, there is also a focus on the correct technique for writing letters and numbers, which is a critical skill for our students to write clearly and effectively communicate their ideas and thoughts while also keeping the writing process smooth and simple.

Figure 8.1. Scan this page using the NarratorAR app.

As I mentioned in Chapter 1, my youngest daughter, Elliana, has dyslexia. It didn't take me long to see how this app might benefit her. She tended to write most of her letters from the bottom up, which I thought was interesting. It should have been an early indication to me that she might have dyslexia, but at the time I thought her way of writing was just her style. I recall my own experience in school, being drilled on the correct way to write each letter and number, but it wasn't until I became mother to a daughter who has dyslexia that I realized how important correct letter writing is for students to become great writers.

In addition to the support for correct letter-writing technique in the NarratorAR app, students are also supported by an enormous library of content. Understanding that students have different needs and preferences for learning, NarratorAR covers the foundational fine motor skills for writing by having students learn the skill, apply the skill, and then build confidence in the skill. Students work on literacy and numeracy in forty ABC and 123 AR activities. Students apply the skills they've learned in the Get Moving and Story Pages AR activities, while building confidence in the Super Hero and Ocean AR adventures. Scan the image in Figure 8.1 in the NarratorAR app to see an example.

Sesgoritma (Sign Language)

Sesgoritma is a mobile sign language translator app powered by artificial intelligence. The app is among the first of the new AR applications that use AI to support communication. Sesgoritma translates sign language by hand tracking in real time using the camera on a device. The purpose of the tool is to minimize barriers when communicating with deaf or hard of hearing (HoH) individuals.

The app works in several ways to support communication and provide knowledge to all individuals. A basic option is speech-to-text, where an individual can speak, and the text will show up on the screen.

While not perfect, Sesgoritma does offer some communication support to individuals who need assistance and don't have access to an interpreter. For the person trying to understand sign language, the app opens the camera and translates some basic signs. The app then converts the signs to text and speaks the text aloud.

The best feature of Sesgoritma is the option to upload your own signs into the app. The app opens the camera and snaps a picture of your sign and its meaning to include in future communication. The app remains imperfect, showing the wrong words at times, but the concept is vitally important, and the AI will improve over time.

Personalized Experiences for All Students

As an aside, one of my best friends, Dr. Marialice Curran, has brought attention to deaf and HoH accessibility in education. Her husband Sean is deaf, and the insight into the obstacles he faces every day helps inform us as we do our part to break down as many barriers as possible. Sean has the amazing ability to read lips to communicate with others outside of the deaf and HoH community. During the COVID-19 pandemic, one of the greatest hardships he faced was the dilemma of masks, which prevented him from reading the lips of anyone wearing one. When his wife saw the possibility of including a transparent film in a mask, our mutual friend Joy Schwartz was up to the challenge of crafting transparent masks for the whole family.

DIY Face Shield
Download the free 3D object to print at bit.ly/printfacemask.

Figure 8.2. Transparent masks like this one allow the deaf and hard of hearing communities the opportunity to read lips. View a 3D version of a face shield that uses cling film (saran wrap) and a rubber band by scanning the QR code (or going to mywebar.com/pi/4737) on a mobile device and then viewing this image.

Microsoft Immersive Reader and MERGE Explorer (Reluctant Readers)

The goal of Microsoft Immersive Reader is to make reading more interactive, translating to better comprehension. The tool provides access to content by customizing text into multiple formats in order to provide a personalized reading arrangement for the individual. The text can be modified by size, font type, font color, highlight color, and spacing based on the students' individual needs. In addition to font adjustments, Immersive Reader will read the text at varying speeds in more than eighty languages, making the content more accessible than ever. If you're still not convinced, Immersive Reader can also convert text into pictures or highlight different parts of speech.

You may be surprised that the Immersive Reader product was initially built for students who have dyslexia. Using Immersive Reader can help level the playing field for struggling readers, making our lessons more equitable for all learners. Additionally, providing a tool that allows our students to be more independent while exploring content is key for them to feel confident in their skills. This tool has supported many students beyond those with dyslexia, because all students can benefit personalizing their reading experiences.

The integration of Immersive Reader in the MERGE Explorer app was released in late 2019. The integration of the content with an immersive experience is an obvious improvement for many learners. But when the content is customized for each individual, readers are able to explore the text and 3D experience with precision to absorb a greater amount of knowledge while deepening their understanding.

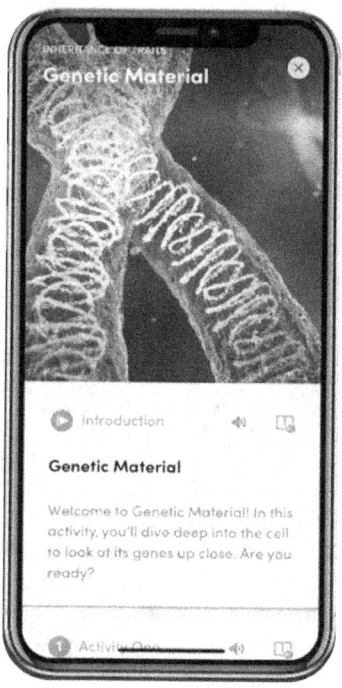

Figure 8.3. Discover what's possible using the MERGE Explorer app with Microsoft's Immersive Reader by scanning this figure using the Arloopa app.

The MERGE team may have integrated Immersive Reader early, but other immersive technology companies are quickly joining in. Nearpod and Flipgrid are other early adopters making content customizable for learners.

NuEyes (Visually Impaired)

The increased enthusiasm for VR in recent years has mainly stemmed from the affordability of the products, which are finally priced for the consumer market. The products have continued to improve in visual clarity, sharpness, and alignment of movement. The medical field has found VR devices extremely beneficial for certain communities.

The NuEyes project has found VR headsets to be especially useful for visually impaired individuals. Using incredible technology, NuEyes transforms the view through a VR headset and provides the means to lighten, clarify, zoom in, change color, and more to give an individual sight! The stories of individuals getting to see for the first time (or for the first time in many years) are overwhelming. VR technology is providing something so much more important than the thrill of a game.

Example: VR with Visually Impaired Students

An example of an educator using VR with visually impaired students comes from Christy Cate at the Region 14 Education Service Center in Abilene, Texas. Cate's center held a pirate-themed adventure titled "Tech Treasures" for their visually impaired students. The makerspace hosted the students and provided many different technology opportunities, and AR/VR was among the students' favorites.

One of the experiences that took the Region 14 team by surprise was the introduction of Google Expeditions and the MERGE Cube. The students were asked to take off their glasses and put on the VR viewer with the Expeditions app for underwater adventure. Many students were hesitant to take off their glasses, because several of the students were legally blind and could only recognize light and color. When the students agreed to try the technology, most of them were able to see things that they'd been unable to before (see an example in Figure 8.4). Using the viewers, students were able to learn in new ways. The experience filled them with laughter and wonder.

Figure 8.4. Scan the QR code using your device camera and then view the image to see some of the sea life that the students were able to discover. How many fish can you find?

Starlight (Medical Procedures)

An organization that has been around in children's hospitals for years is the Starlight charity, which has sought to bring many smiles to seriously ill children. The organization has brought interactive gaming spaces into the hospitals, so children and parents can escape for a bit from the burdens that they face. Starlight has continued with their mission for many years and has recently begun introducing VR into hospitals. The responses from the children have been stunning and have encouraged Starlight to continue providing more than 1,300 VR headsets in the hospitals for more children to enjoy.

The Starlight organization has found that VR gives children the illusion that they are being transported to a new world. Samsung headsets are preloaded with twenty applications for children to select from. The devices allow children to use them lying down or sitting up, making the experience accessible for the various needs of the individual. In some cases, the VR experience has been so powerful, it has reduced the need for certain medications in some children.

It's an incredible feeling to know that immersive technology can convince your body that you've been transported to another place, so much so that children feel safer and happier. The impact of immersive experiences on these children's mental health is also positive, reducing the anxiety and trauma that hospitalized children often experience and changing the way they feel about medical care.

Limbix (Depression)

New technology in immersive mental health is being developed to support adolescent children who struggle with depression. Limbix technology uses VR for cognitive behavior therapy and provides value-based activities to provide digital therapeutic interventions. Limbix may allow youth to find ways to cope with stress, anxiety, and depression outside of prescription drugs. While this treatment is still in its early stages, it's important to note that the medical field values the impact that VR can have, and these interventions will continue to grow in the coming years.

One Size Does Not Fit All

Approaching the selection and use of AR/VR tools, the educator should recognize that some students will need different experiences than others. To give every student an iPad or Chromebook and think they will all thrive on that device is just as ridiculous as saying they will all love the same subject in school. Not only will they have different preferences, but they'll have diverse needs and skills. The different devices have specific uses and purposes and when identifying which device is needed, ideally we should look at individual students.

If we learned anything from the COVID-19 global pandemic, it was that the ability to provide quality remote learning is critical. One of the biggest areas of concern initially was the limited availability of resources for our students to learn from home. The schools that were already set up with 1:1 devices were impacted by the pandemic shutdown, but not nearly as much as those schools that didn't have devices or access for their students.

While the discussion for 1:1 devices in schools has been around for more than a decade, the budgets to purchase and maintain those devices are rarely available. Schools that were able to purchase devices were often funded through grants, and when it was time to replace the devices, there was no funding to upgrade with new devices. Now that schools have seen how the pandemic has impacted student learning, many are attempting to prepare for the future. This is the time to make the needs of individual students a top priority to deliver exceptional learning at school or remotely.

Student Ownership

The products and activities that we use in the classroom rarely originate from students. Students have little say about classroom products because they are not included in the purchasing discussion. We can guess what we believe students will want to use in their learning, and it's possible that we may guess correctly. However, the best way to approach choosing student products and activities is to invite our students into the discussion.

Evaluating past student work can provide good insight into a new product. What is the product capable of doing, and can it meet the needs of my individual learners? Do the student products inspire ideas for your lessons, or do they seem limited? Is the immersive technology tool purposeful when exploring in AR/VR, or is it just a gimmick? Do the final results of the program require the immersive technology aspect, or does it just add to the experience as entertainment? These are important questions to ask when considering a new product or program. Including student feedback can help inform your decision making by understanding how your students envision using the product in their learning.

Many schools are engaged with companies that are eager for you to test their product, and if given the opportunity, classrooms can get early access to an upcoming tool, provide feedback to deliver the best product to the classroom, and get top-notch support while using the new product for free. Most immersive technology companies are new start-ups who need pilot schools to help them define the final product while also getting valuable insight into the needs and interests of the classroom. When districts are testing new products or programs, ask students to be part of that testing process. These beta testers will love being the first to experience new products. Most importantly, we show these students that their voices are important—their suggestions may inform the design of these products for other classrooms.

Student Voice and Choice

Lake Shore Central Schools in Angola, New York, provided a great example of schools using the latest tools with students' interests in mind. The technology integration specialist, Michael Drezek, worked with the high school art teachers to support an initiative to bring 3D design into the classroom using Google Tilt Brush. Based on the New York state media art standards, students were asked to create, perform, produce, respond to, and present artwork. The goal of using Google Tilt

Brush was to empower students to meet media art standards as well as the ISTE Standards for Students. Through a team planning approach, the learning experience included Google Tilt Brush on the Oculus Rift, Screencastify, and Google Classroom.

A strategic technology plan and a responsible budget allowed the district to purchase VR headsets. The purchase granted students the ability to creatively demonstrate knowledge using Tilt Brush on the Oculus Rift, shared in Google Poly. The art included famous historical pieces and original artwork. The VR learning experience demonstrated the incredible talent and diverse skills that each student brought to the project.

Steps Taken by LSCS to Use Tilt Brush in the Art Classroom

- Plan the right technology to meet the goals and objectives.
- Identify possible devices and programs and research educational uses.
- Purchase Oculus Rift.
- Purchase and install Tilt Brush by Google.
- Collaborate with the IT Department to work through any web filtering issues.
- Get familiar with the device and application.
- Watch and enjoy students creating art in virtual reality.
- Be willing and ready to get "unstuck" when faced with something new.
- Export creations to Google Poly to share work with an authentic audience (without providing the full names of the students).
- Teach students how to use Screencastify.
- Teach students how to share files to Google Classroom.
- Learn from one another, side by side.
- Celebrate each other's successes.
- Gather feedback from students and brainstorm new ways to utilize VR in the art classroom.

After completing the projects, students were trusted to use their experience and create Tilt Brush tutorials for their peers. The tutorials were filled with the students' process in their artwork, as well as insight into new ways to use Tilt Brush, and were then posted in Google Classroom. The learning experience allowed students and teachers to work side by side using immersive technology. Drezek believes in the power of creation and recommends that students lead when using these technologies:

> You don't need to be an expert to get started. You just need to be a willing learner and open to the possibilities of what AR and VR could bring to your classroom to meet learning objectives.

The immersive journey that Lake Shore Central Schools went through was highly successful and at times had unexpected occurrences. The plan and objectives were clear and completed, but there were other outcomes that the team experienced along the way. In an effort to receive the maximum benefit from these immersive lessons, there was flexibility to allow the experience to expand beyond its specific purpose, providing educators and students new and creative ways to use the tool.

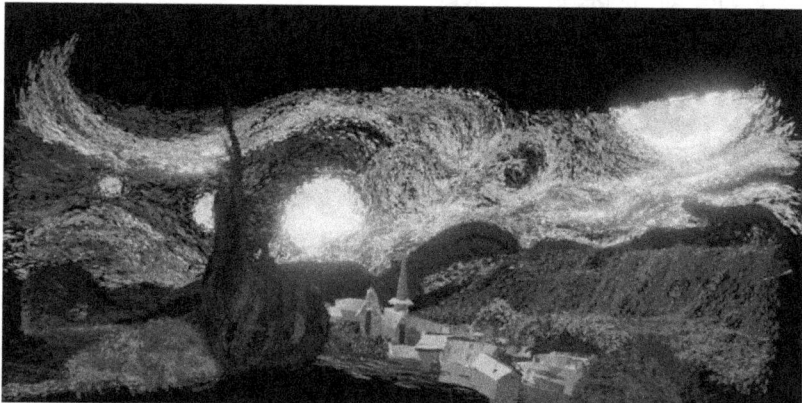

Figure 8.5. View this Google Tilt Brush creation by scanning the QR code and selecting View AR in the ARize app.

Passion-Based Learning

My good friend Andi McNair is an expert on Genius Hour, or passion-based learning. Her work with gifted and talented students was the start of her journey, but she believes that every student deserves the opportunity to pursue their passion in learning. She works with schools to implement the genius hour process with learners to impact others and inspire change.

In her presentations, she often delivers examples of immersive technology as a compelling option for students to experience new places and increase engagement, improving a willingness to invest into the project. One of the top resources include AR portals to allow students to walk into new places and explore the world from anywhere using AR. Andi presents the benefits of using the MERGE Cube to visualize objects needed to explore in the student projects. Using immersive technology, she encourages a commitment to extend learning in ways that are impossible without it.

Student Leadership

At times, we think we know exactly what our students need and want in immersive technology, but until we present it to our students, we're only taking a guess. I've often felt excited to share a new resource with students only to find that they don't place the same value on that experience as I did. On the other hand, I've given students a tool to test out expecting it to be a flop only to have them love using it. The students have much more enthusiasm to continue exploring than I could have imagined. In the end, we need our students to guide us to use the best and most effective tools while maintaining their interest with challenges and active learning experiences.

An incredibly talented member of the ARVRinEDU community is David Lockett. If there is something new being developed, David has already tried it with his STEM students. Mr. Lockett's passion to bring in new tools is motivated by his students' enthusiasm for learning. The direction of the classroom is largely led by his students as he's empowered them to pursue their passions by exposing them to many areas of STEM.

The use of immersive technology is an engaging method to capture the interests of our students. He believes that AR and VR apps go beyond the "cool" factor to foster skills that are in high demand for new careers ranging from construction to healthcare. In the STEM classroom, he believes that AR/VR tools provide the visual learning that many students need to make a deeper connection to the content while capturing their attention and sparking their imagination. In short, immersive technology is much more than "wow."

In Mr. Lockett's classroom, he has the unique opportunity to introduce relevant AR and VR content and concepts to build students' design thinking, problem-solving, and critical analysis skills. The use of immersive technology supports the needed learning experiences without the high cost. Valuable mobile content eliminates the learning curve and the requirement to purchase new products.

Immersive Learning Challenge

Ask your students to create a video tutorial on an immersive technology tool that will support all learners. Share the link to the video tutorial on social media using #ARVRinEDU.

Personalizing Professional Development

An important detail that's often overlooked when implementing immersive technology is the absolute necessity for professional development. Most schools purchase AR/VR technology without considering how to equip teachers to effectively use the tools. Additionally, the companies selling the products often don't offer much support specific to education, as the products are mainly intended for average consumers. Professional development is essential for providing the necessary support to effectively integrate AR/VR products into your curriculum.

After sharing AR/VR tools with educators for many years, I've learned that teachers often need more than a single presentation—or multiple presentations, for that matter—to really feel confident about exploring and putting to use the available tools. Teachers need opportunities to engage with the tool within a safe and collaborative community in order to receive support when they make mistakes or run into problems. Most educators will resist using any new technology with students until they feel comfortable using it themselves.

Not only should collaboration and training be part of the plan when implementing AR/VR, but it's also important to provide training well before making final decisions on purchases, if possible. On many occasions, schools have purchased devices and then contacted me about providing training. Often these purchases were made via sales representatives who made recommendations based on the greatest financial gain for their company. You'll find that nearly all of the AR/VR product recommendations in this book aren't available through distributors because the profit is simply too small for them to put in the effort. My point is: the most effective immersive technology tools available for the classroom are quite often very cost effective. Providing training prior to purchase will help weed out the (possibly expensive) AR/VR products that aren't what teachers want or need.

Personalized Learning for Educators

Like students, educators benefit from a personalized approach to learning these new technologies. Mandating that a tool be used in every classroom without preparing the educator to properly use the tool is setting up the teacher and the tool for failure. Allowing freedom for educators to explore and use the appropriate tools—those that fit their students' needs as well as their own—is important. Providing the training and flexibility to make the tools work for different classrooms and educators is the best approach.

A good relationship between classroom teachers and those supporting educational technology on the campus is vital. When serving as an instructional technologist, I found that my main job wasn't providing forgotten logins or helping open up a grade book, but rather was building a relationship of trust and support with each of the educators on my campuses. Establishing genuine trust will create the best atmosphere for supporting those educators in their AR/VR journey.

My background in teaching math ranges from ages four to fourteen in rural, urban, and suburban populations. I've taught in public and private schools and coached girls' sports for schools and private clubs. The one constant for teaching in these different settings remained the same: it was all about relationships. I found my greatest satisfaction in teaching students who struggled most with math. My last classroom teaching position was working with students who had failed the standardized tests. Similiarly I find that I am drawn to those educators who struggle the most with technology. All teachers can implement this exciting technology. It takes a willingness to encourage, support, and uplift those educators who give it a try. Flexibility in your training methods is key.

Personalized learning must apply to our educators' professional development as much as it applies to our students. We've all been to the professional development sessions where we spent an entire day learning a program that cost the district a fortune, being told that we must use this program every day only to notice that the tool isn't mentioned again for the remainder of the year. This is obviously bad professional development practice.

My preference for training always includes a hands-on approach in both individual and group settings. Covering content as a group and then moving to independent work is the way we often approach our students' learning. We get to understand our students as individuals, and then present material in a variety of ways to meet their many needs. I find that some educators resist engaging in professional development exercises. The problem often is that we've not captured what's most important to that educator, so they feel that topic isn't worth the energy. When we can connect the reasons for using immersive technology to the needs of the educator, most find they are driven to learn for the benefit of their students.

Every teacher will bring with them a variety of good and bad past technology experiences and a wide range of skills. Getting familiar with a teacher's background can be the first step in building trust. If an educator is struggling to connect AR/VR to their curriculum, ask other teachers to provide inspirational ideas. If you notice that a teacher is distracted by her phone, ask her to become part of the demonstration by showcasing the technology on her mobile device. The good news about most immersive technology is that you rarely get a lack of enthusiasm after teachers get a snapshot of the capabilities of AR/VR.

Connect the tools to the interests of the educator. There is a plethora of applications; most anyone can locate and learn a tool that resonates with them. In one presentation, I had an educator who was an avid gardener, and while I was showing an AR creation tool, she smiled when she saw the variety of plants within the app. When I saw her interest, I decided to demonstrate the technology by creating an AR planter box in the room. She was thrilled because she was presenting at a gardeners' conference the following week and, after the experience in the training, planned to show the app to participants. As soon as she connected the technology with her own interest, she was hooked for the remainder of the session. Find similar ways to captivate your teachers-in-training.

Steve Bambury, from Dubai, is a trailblazer in educational AR/VR technology. In 2017 he created a pioneering form of professional development by hosting an event titled CPD (Continuing Professional Development) on a newer (at the time) VR platform called Engage. I was honored to be included in the first panel discussion, on the topic of AR/VR in education. At the time, I had only my computer to join in the experience. Even so, once I was on the stage and speaking with these amazing individuals, I was completely captivated by the immersive experience. In addition to Steve as host, myself, and the other panelists, a decent-sized group was part of the audience. The whole experience was a bit surreal.

I believe Engage was creating the right platform at the right time. Bambury was able to envision global collaboration via a VR platform that wasn't quite ready for the general population but was well on its way to becoming part of the future of communication. It was Bambury's hope to begin using VR with his students, but because of school device limitations, he decided to focus on educator professional development instead.

As you may have guessed, the CPD events took off, and Bambury continues to host events on the Engage platform. His audience has grown to include many leading immersive technology industry professionals and the conversations are rich with important topics that provide insight into the future of AR/VR. Learn more on his website, engagevr.io/tag/steve-bambury.

Building Community with ARVRinEDU

Several years ago, I felt the need to begin having targeted discussions on AR/VR in education. Most existing discussions at the time were focused on consumer use and targeted to avid tech gurus. Incredible resources were beginning to be revealed, and as these tools were released, I was researching and immediately sharing them out in presentations or on social media. The desire to begin an online community was actually born in 2016 during a virtual event using the platform Voxer called EdCampVoxer. To get the conversation started, I created a Voxer group called VRinEDU but quickly changed it to ARVRinEDU when the discussion kept bringing up augmented reality. I realized that both technologies were immersive and important, and that the discussion shouldn't separate the two.

Prior to this event, I was thinking about starting a regular Twitter chat on the topic of AR/VR in education, but I knew this was a serious commitment because I would need to be consistent and post questions every week to keep the discussion going long term. When the first #ARVRinEDU chat began on November 9, 2016, I was terrified that I was the only educator that would show up. I was incredibly grateful to the educators that joined and shared in the first #ARVRinEDU chat and helped spread the word.

The first #ARVRinEDU chat posed this question for discussion: "Where are we going with AR & VR?" The resulting conversations addressed how to identify AR versus VR and how both could be used in the classroom. The second chat was hosted by CoSpaces, which only provided VR at the time. The third chat was hosted by Sarah Thomas, who brought up collaboration and AR/VR creation tools. After the first month, I decided to turn the #ARVRinEDU chat into mini-PD lessons.

Discussion topics would come up occasionally, but I wanted educators to walk away learning a new tool that they could apply the following week. Not too long after starting the chat, I decided to cut the time down from one hour to thirty minutes, which has remained the standard ever since.

For the past few years, I've collected and shared a year's worth of #ARVRinEDU chat highlights. Access 2018 and 2019 resources and highlights by scanning Figures 9.1 and 9.2 below. These blog posts include the top tweets from each week. I intended to give those that missed some chats access to materials and links for new tools. Not only are there many resources for getting started with immersive technology in the classroom, but the community members that engaged with the content via #ARVRinEDU are the greatest—so knowledgeable and willing to help.

The connections I've made via the #ARVRinEDU chat are now lifetime friends. These educators share the same passion—to see education thriving using emerging technologies like AR/VR. The community is quite special as the individuals range in subject, grade level, position, and skill level. Each person brings a different specialty, and everyone is quick to support others by answering questions or inspiring ideas. The impact of implementing immersive technology by yourself will likely be limited, but with a connection to the #ARVRinEDU community, you and those around you will benefit.

Joining the weekly #ARVRinEDU Twitter chat is easy.

1. Go to Twitter.com and sign up for an account (for new accounts).
2. Type the hashtag #ARVRinEDU in the search bar.
3. Select Latest to see the most recent posts using the hashtag #ARVRinEDU.
4. Posts will show up in this feed when it includes the hashtag #ARVRinEDU.
5. Questions will begin with Q1, Q2, Q3, and your answers to the questions will respond with A1, A2, A3, and so on.
6. Reply to answers coming from the community.
7. Follow the educators in the chat to continue learning and put the new tools into practice.

THE IMMERSIVE CLASSROOM

ARVRinEDU.com and Blog

After the start of the weekly Twitter chat, I was getting regular requests for information. I would share a video or link to an app along the way, but the need was growing to have one place where I could direct everyone for a compilation of content. The ARVRinEDU.com domain was purchased at the beginning of 2017 and I began to develop the website.

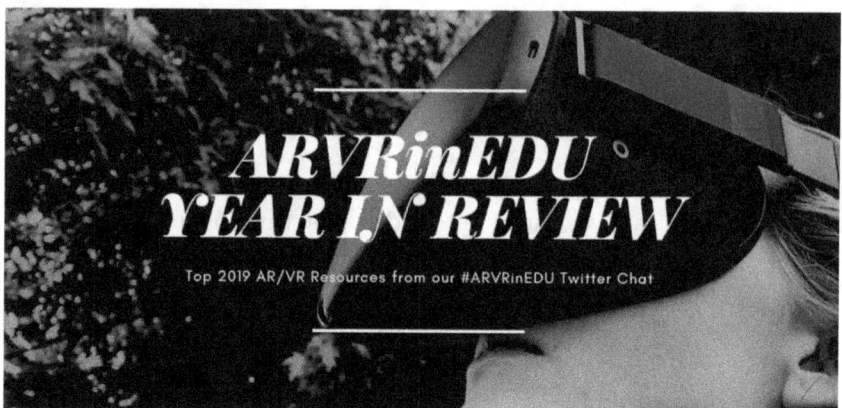

Figure 9.1. View the 2019 Top Resources by scanning this image using the ARize app to get the link to the resources.

Figure 9.2. View the 2018 Top Resources by scanning this image using the ARize app to get the link to the resources.

ARVRinEDU.com provides access to videos, links to some of my publications, contact information, and most importantly, my blog. Posting the latest updates on immersive technology tools for the classroom is my passion. The blog connects practical resources with substantial benefits for our learners. At times, I post articles for other publications, and when permission is granted, I cross-post this content on my blog, allowing all the content to be housed in one location.

I am very careful of the way I present immersive technology. You'll notice the content is relatable and described in understandable terms. Getting into the complexity of immersive technology isn't always necessary, especially when recommending classroom tools. The technology is described in simple, straightforward language that outlines each tool's benefits, potential problems, and how to use it most effectively and safely with students. The ARVRinEDU blog typically includes a video tutorial containing explanations and step-by-step directions. The website also provides an integrated search feature for locating specific content.

#31DaysofARVRinEDU

The time of year that I find things slow down considerably for ARVRinEDU is during the month of March. I believe this has quite a bit to do with the timing of standardized tests throughout the US. Around this time, I work hard to get caught up on projects or launching new ideas that have been on pause during the busy conference seasons. One project that started in March of 2019 was the start of an annual event called #31DaysofARVRinEDU.

The goal of #31DaysofARVRinEDU was to spend the month of March building content on the blog. I posted a new tool or significant update every day during the month, providing visual and video resources, direct links to resources, and directions on using each tool effectively in the classroom. My slowest month of the year thus became my busiest month, but the excitement from the ARVRinEDU community has encouraged me to continue the #31DaysofARVRinEDU event.

All ARVRinEDU.com subscribers receive daily emails of new posts and other important immersive technology updates throughout the year. The posts are also shared on social media using the hashtag #31DaysofARVRinEDU. At the completion of the blog posts in March, I share an infographic (see Figure 9.3) of all the resources covered with hyperlinks to the blog posts.

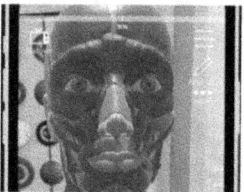

Figure 9.3. Infographic for #31DaysofARVRinEDU. Access the post with the linked infographic at bit.ly/31daysofarvrinedu or by scanning the QR code. You may want to bookmark the page for reference and for learning more about each of the tools featured.

The Immersive Experience

Many educators discover resources and tools at educational conferences. The opportunity to select the perfect sessions for your individual needs is ideal—the sessions include speakers on a variety of topics, subjects, and grade levels. Having a dedicated time for professional growth while building deeper connections with your team and new educators is an opportunity that many educators hope to get. There are many conferences for educators around the world, and most now include the chance to learn more about augmented and virtual reality.

I've found the best practices to inspire and avoid overwhelming the educator consist of providing practical ways to bring the technology into the classroom. Recently at various conferences, a new way to present AR/VR learning was provided to deliver a more personalized experience for the educator through exploring tools in an interactive, hands-on learning experience. I've dubbed these events the Immersive Experience.

STATION 1
MINECRAFT EARTH
Collect items and build an augmented reality space. Join a friend to build together.

STATION 2
AR PORTALS
Create an augmented reality portal and walk in and out of the 360.

iOS Android

iOS Android

Figure 9.4. The Immersive Experience provides personalized PD. View these images using the Arloopa app to learn more about Minecraft Earth and AR Portals.

These experiences are set up with 6–8 stations that include a variety of AR/VR tools. Each station has a specific task to perform to give the educator a complete view of the tool's capabilities while walking them through how to use it. Immersive Experiences begin at the check-in location, where a flyer with station tasks is provided (see Figure 9.4). Each station has a volunteer to help the educator understand and complete the task, and when completed, the volunteer provides a stamp on the flyer. The teacher can go to the stations in any order but must complete all the stations and receive stamps for every task before returning to the check-in location to receive an ARVRinEDU goodie bag.

Out of all my past presentations, I've received more enthusiasm about this type of learning experience because it was challenging and fun at the same time. The teachers enjoyed learning about the latest tools firsthand, and testing the tools gave them the confidence to immediately put them into practice. The ARVRinEDU goodie bags were incentives for educators to complete all the tasks, while also providing the tools to begin using AR/VR.

Each time I've delivered the Immersive Experience, I've made changes to the tools at the different stations. I've also modified the tasks to fit the time frame needed to keep up the energy and flow of the experience. The teachers and volunteers change at each event but the excitement to learn remains. Get a glimpse of the Immersive Experience from a video recorded by Marialice Curran at TCEA in 2020. Scan the image in Figure 9.5 to watch the video.

#ARVRinEDU: Train the Trainer

Over the years, as I've presented and consulted on immersive technology, I've received many requests to go into greater depth, specifically for those individuals who plan to train other educators on this technology. To answer these requests, I began offering a two-day training that covers the foundation and the details of many AR/VR tools. The training also covered curriculum connections and the most effective approaches when using immersive technology in the classroom.

This extensive training provided resources, links, and detailed notes for the attendees to use in future training. The two-day training gave the educators the tools needed to get started, such as trial subscriptions, MERGE Cube, MERGE headset, and a copy of my book *Learning Transported*. These tools were used throughout the training and allowed the teachers to first test out and then dive into the immersive experiences. The book provided the foundation on the concepts and examples of practical applications in the classroom.

Figure 9.5. Learn more about this Immersive Experience from an interview with Marialice Curran. Scan this image using the ARize app.

Immersive Technology in Social Media

The way we connect across the world has changed drastically in the past decade. Our social media channels usually consist of more than one platform and often include personal as well as professional discussions. Our educational norm went from condemning social media to asking educators to use it for professional development. My professional journey would look much different if I had never used social media to connect and share. Many wonderful professional growth opportunities have emerged since educators began using Twitter, Facebook, Instagram, and more.

Social media companies have recognized a massive market for augmented and virtual reality. Their initial inclusion of immersive technology began with the introduction of 360-degree images and videos users could view in social media posts. Users were able to load pictures and videos taken on a 360-degree camera or from their mobile devices using 360-degree apps. Having the option to scroll around and explore in 360 degrees was much more appealing than a standard image or video.

Following this VR integration, the use of AR face filters became popular for users of all ages. I believe the interest in AR filters stems from the creative options to express yourself and the added benefit of generating illusions. Since AR filters seem real, students can playfully become the character. The saying that "a picture is worth a thousand words" is truer in AR filters than traditional images on social media because the view is often extreme or unrealistic.

The latest integration of immersive technology targets hardware with VR standalone headset devices. When Facebook purchased the virtual reality company, Oculus, there was no doubt that the social media giant was anticipating a new era of global collaboration.

The first standalone device released by Oculus ignited a new revolution of affordable VR headsets for consumers. Many of the other headsets had such a high starting price point that the average consumer couldn't afford them. The Oculus Go essentially had the user sit down and look around them using a single remote to select a new place to stand. I found some people got motion sickness from this experience mainly because of the quality of the graphics, but also because the body is never actually moving to those locations, rather transporting within the virtual space. The technology for the Oculus Go is 3DoF, meaning it affords three degrees of freedom—the user can look around left to right, look up, and look down using the Oculus Go, but can't walk around.

A much-improved headset arrived with the release of the Oculus Quest in April 2019. The realistic interactions turned the Quest into an incredible standalone device at a reasonable price. The 6DoF (six degrees of freedom) allow the user to not only look around, but walk forward and backward and jump up or squat down. The Quest also includes two remotes, but recently released an update for hand tracking to serve as the remote for the device. In the Oculus store, the apps are mainly geared for gaming and entertainment, but educational opportunities are growing rapidly. One of the best current uses of the VR headsets is collaboration and creation, with the opportunity to easily connect and build together in a virtual space being an impressive feature.

I believe the greatest VR growth will be available in our browsers. The cross-platform approach is wise for companies trying to get the largest audience, and it's exceptionally beneficial for schools that are limited by devices. Since the technology lives in the browser, students and educators can join using their phone, tablet, computer, or VR headset to access the site, making the experience much richer and available to anyone regardless of the device used to participate.

ISTE Standards for Educators

For compelling reasons to consider using VR for collaboration, look no further than the ISTE Standards for Educators. As learners, educators want to continue growing by connecting with and learning from other educators. Ultimately, these practices will directly affect students, as your methods, resources, and strategies improve by learning from and with others around the world.

Following are examples of how AR/VR can help meet the ISTE Standards for Educators.

1. **Learner. Educators continually improve their practice by learning from and with others and exploring proven and promising practices that leverage technology to improve student learning.**

    b. Pursue professional interests by creating and actively participating in local and global learning networks.

As an educational leader, the use of VR to connect with others provides a model for your students to do the same. Students will view, explore, and create in the virtual meeting spaces based on their preference and interests.

2. **Leader. Educators seek out opportunities for leadership to support student empowerment and success and to improve teaching and learning.**

    b. Advocate for equitable access to educational technology, digital content and learning opportunities to meet the diverse needs of all students.

A VR meeting space opens up many opportunities for collaboration. It's the responsibility of the educator to lead students in productive, honorable conversations in the digital world—conversations that will impact the classroom, the community, and the world.

3. **Citizen. Educators inspire students to positively contribute to and responsibly participate in the digital world.**

    a. Create experiences for learners to make positive, socially responsible contributions and exhibit empathetic behavior online that build relationships and community.

There is no debate regarding the benefits of student collaboration in the classroom. Learning from others and with others is key. The same benefit holds true for educators as they learn from and with their peers and their students. VR meeting spaces allow for more authentic discussions and gives students the freedom to have multiple chats around the room. The option to add 3D objects, presentation slides, and drawings when discussing content makes the interactions much more beneficial than a video chat.

4. **Collaborator.** Educators dedicate time to collaborate with both colleagues and students to improve practice, discover and share resources and ideas, and solve problems.

   c. Use collaborative tools to expand students' authentic, real-world learning experiences by engaging virtually with experts, teams and students, locally and globally.

There's no doubt that VR meeting spaces capture and engage our learners. Each VR meeting platform includes multiple spaces to select or create, allowing the class to make the environment conducive to the needs of all learners.

5. **Designer.** Educators design authentic, learner-driven activities and environments that recognize and accommodate learner variability.

   c. Explore and apply instructional design principles to create innovative digital learning environments that engage and support learning.

The flexibility of VR meeting spaces can benefit a variety of educational settings. The educator can coordinate a schedule with a targeted audience for specific educational needs. As a developer of the space, it's important for educators to share how to use and create VR meeting spaces.

6. **Facilitator.** Educators facilitate learning with technology to support student achievement of the ISTE Standards for Students.

   b. Manage the use of technology and student learning strategies in digital platforms, virtual environments, hands-on makerspaces or in the field.

As students move around independently in VR meeting spaces, they determine how to connect and create to effectively share knowledge of the content. An incredible alternative to a typical document or slide is opening a virtual space to expand the classroom walls and bring experiences that are otherwise impossible in a classroom.

7. **Analyst.** Educators understand and use data to drive their instruction and support students in achieving their learning goals.

   a. Provide alternative ways for students to demonstrate competency and reflect on their learning using technology.

Personalizing Professional Development

Figure 9.6. Learn about this Mozilla Hubs Halloween meeting space by scanning the image with the Arloopa app. Join this VR space at hub.link/yPZt4wE and try to complete the challenges.

VR Meeting Spaces

For the past few years, I've been intrigued with VR meeting spaces, as they offer a more realistic way to connect with people around the world. The virtual space kept up my interest and enthusiasm to learn, leading to increased retention on my part. I've always been eager to find these spaces offered on multiple device types. This is especially true in education since so many classrooms don't have VR headsets. Many cross-platform resources have been released in the recent past, arriving just in time to prove useful for the COVID-19 pandemic.

Mozilla Hubs

I first encountered Mozilla Hubs when exploring tools for the #31DaysofARVR inEDU event. The ease of use, device compatibility, interactive options, and realistic collaboration offered by Mozilla Hubs is a big win for schools, especially those implementing remote learning. Mozilla Hubs provides several VR meeting space templates to bring in a classroom quickly without requiring any code. The creator of the room can easily share the link to the virtual meeting space by going to hub.link and providing the six-digit code.

THE IMMERSIVE CLASSROOM

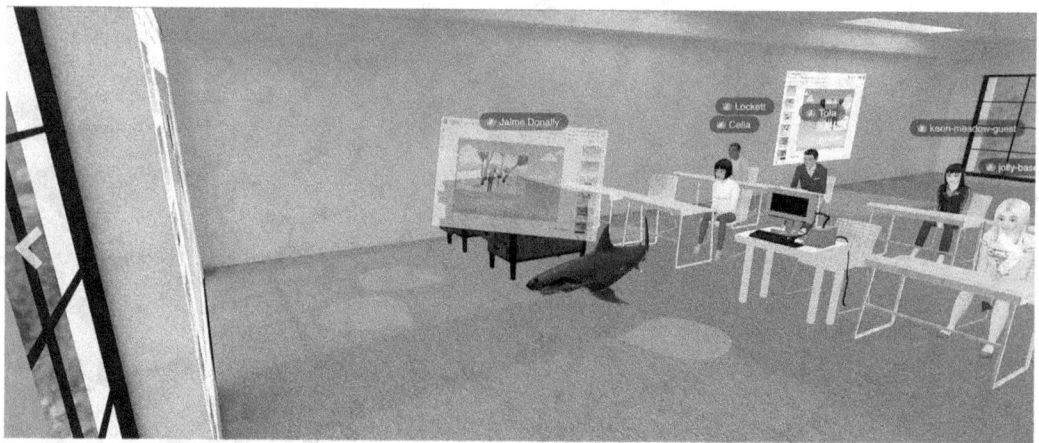

Figure 9.7. Join this VR meeting space by going to bit.ly/learnbriteclass. Click the blue hotspots to move around the room.

As mentioned in Chapter 4, Mozilla Hubs is a WebXR resource, making it completely browser based, which allows for multiple device types to connect, share, and collaborate. Hubs features are perfect for a new user. They include a webcam view, screen share, drawing, camera and video capture, chat, and a library of 3D objects. The best feature in Hubs is the ability to create 3D objects to customize your VR meeting space using Spoke.

Many of these VR spaces limit the number of people joining, because too many participants can cause the experience to slow down or glitch. The recommended maximum size for the space is twenty-five at a time; however, the rooms can host a maximum of fifty participants. I have exceeded that number with more than one hundred participants at a time, but the experience becomes quite unstable when adding too many people at once.

UtopiaVR.io

UtopiaVR uses WebXR to essentially offer all the same functions as Hubs, but with a larger library of meeting space templates. An educator can bring the class to a museum, convention center, office, boardroom, tech center, and more. The experience feels nearly identical to Hubs, but provides more detailed VR spaces, making the experience more intriguing. Similar to Hubs, the suggested maximum attendee limit is twenty-five.

Personalizing Professional Development

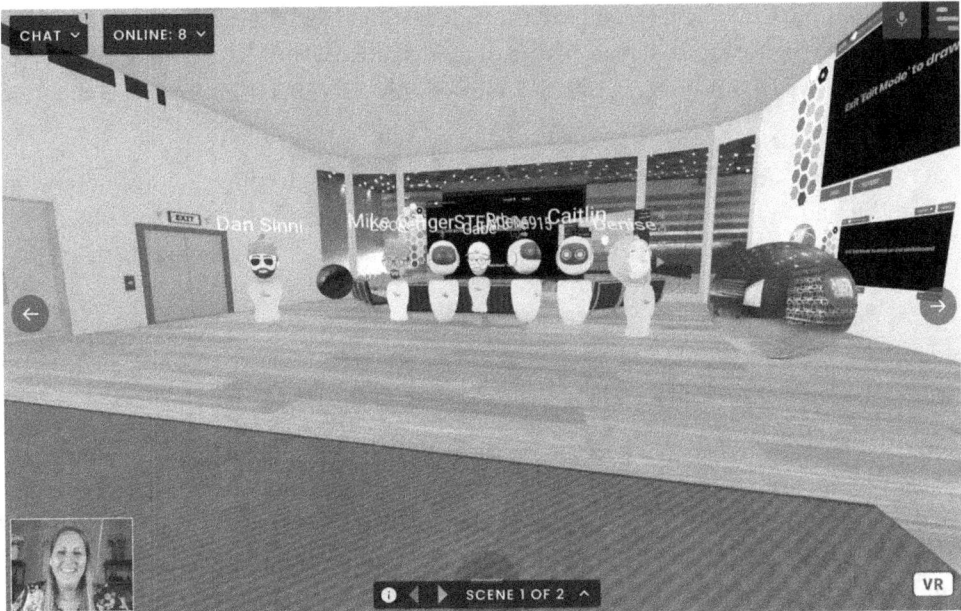

Figure 9.8. Join this VR meeting space in FrameVR at framevr.io/arvrineduchat.

Meetup by Learnbrite

An extremely powerful VR meeting space is Meetup by Learnbrite. The options to customize preferences in Learnbrite are extensive, yet the appearance is presented simply for most commonly used features. Meetup integrates with most other programs. This platform is currently in beta mode, but when the product is fully launched, it appears that it will support a district, campus, or organization for virtual meetings.

FrameVR.io

The FrameVR platform is similar to many of the other WebXR tools but offers a few extra features that make it stand out in some situations. Currently, FrameVR allows for up to thirty individuals at one time, and they are working to make this limit much larger. The company boasts a new VR expo hall which suggests that conferences may be in the near future for FrameVR.

Users can upload 3D objects into their inventory and load them into the scene. Integration with Sketchfab is also available to quickly load 3D objects from the library. To keep the space optimized, FrameVR allows only ten objects in the space at a time.

HAND TRACKING

One big update in FrameVR is the use of hand tracking in the Oculus Quest. The hand tracking feature allows students to use natural gestures to control objects in the scene. The feature is new and improving with each update and is the right next step for this type of technology.

#GlobalMakerDay

Over the past five years, I've had the privilege of hosting a global, collaborative event online. My goal in creating the event was to inspire our classrooms to attempt maker activities and transition our students from consumers to producers of content. Global Maker Day brings in presenters from around the world, while delivering a challenge for students to manufacture while watching.

The virtual event is recorded in Zoom and shown live through the Global Maker Day website. Leveraging social media, the event is shared to classrooms around the world. With a heavy emphasis on collaboration, the organizing team now has the Oculus Quest 2 to connect and plan for the virtual event. Since we each live in different locations around the country, it's impossible to get together in person to plan for Global Maker Day. In VR, the conversations are more immersive as we move about the space, adding and presenting content as if we were sitting in the same room together. It's not always practical to meet in VR, but it does allow us to do much more when we need to ideate.

 Immersive Learning Challenge

Challenge your students to build a VR meeting space that includes uploaded 3D objects, images, and videos. Share the link to the VR meeting space on social media using #ARVRinEDU.

Conclusion

Our classrooms are full of individuals that need to learn in diverse ways. Using immersive technology in our teaching strategies should target students' interest, provide flexibility for a range of skill levels, and empower our students' choice in their learning. Highlighting the possibilities of immersive technology should impact beyond just our core classrooms and reach all student populations.

From our intervention classes to our gifted programs, our students demand the use of creative teaching approaches that would enrich learning for all. Our goal is providing engaging experiences that will deepen learning, while targeting students' specific struggles. Through relationships, educators learn the interests and needs of individual students to provide the best learning environment possible, while inspiring skills for the technology of the future.

The flexibility of the tools must meet the standards at the highest level and create a bridge for students to master the content in immersive activities. Empowering our students with a passion for knowledge is the strength behind augmented and virtual reality. Bringing the learning into the classroom or distance learning environment will require creativity and dedication, but the greatest challenge is captivating our students with a love for learning. The immersive classroom will create, smash, hack, and break out of the lesson restrictions we were once limited by and open a new portal to learning with AR/VR.

Appendix
AR/VR Resources

This appendix shares an index of over 100 AR/VR tools, many of which are free, for you to use in your immersive learning journey. The following table shares the type of tool (AR, VR, or both), whether it can be used for AR/VR creation, the platform (web or browser-based, mobile device, or VR system such as Oculus), recommended subject and grade level, and any requirements such as components needing purchase.

Given the rapidly transforming landscape of immersive technology, these tools are subject to change. Check my website arvrinedu.com for blog posts about new tools or ones that have gone away. Good luck, and happy creating!

NAME	ACCESS	AR/VR	CREATION TOOL?	APP TYPE	SUBJECT	GRADE LEVEL	NEEDS
3D AR Maps by Mapbox	mapbox.com/maps	AR	No	Mobile	Social Studies	K–12	
3DBear	3dbear.io	AR	Yes	Mobile	All	K–12	
3D Paint	Google Play: bit.ly/3raXn0g iOS: apple.co/34r4qYP	AR	Yes	Mobile	Art	K–12	

108

Appendix AR/VR Resources

NAME	ACCESS	AR/VR	CREATION TOOL?	APP TYPE	SUBJECT	GRADE LEVEL	NEEDS
4D Anatomy	4danatomy.com	AR	No	Mobile	Science	K–8	
Adobe Aero	adobe.com/products/aero.html	AR	Yes	Mobile	All	K–12	
Anima Res	animares.com	AR	No	Mobile	Science	6–8	
Apollo 11 HD	bit.ly/34ohX3g	VR	No	VR app	Social studies	3–12	VR headset
ARize	arize.com	AR	Yes	Mobile and web	All	K–12	
ARLOOPA	arloopa.com	AR	Yes	Mobile and web	All	K–12	
Assemblr & Assemblr Studio	assemblrworld.com	AR	Yes	Mobile	All	K–12	

109

THE IMMERSIVE CLASSROOM

NAME	ACCESS	AR/VR	CREATION TOOL?	APP TYPE	SUBJECT	GRADE LEVEL	NEEDS
AugmentifyIt	bit.ly/2KADkaK	AR	No	Mobile	Science	K–5	Cards
BBC Civilisa-tionsAR	Google Play: bit.ly/2LmW7q9 iOS: apple.co/3779F1C	AR	No	Mobile	Social Studies	K–12	
Beat Saber	beatsaber.com	VR	No	VR app	Physical Education	K–12	VR headset
Catchy Words AR	Android: bit.ly/3mgBp8s iOS: apple.co/3oMNEef	AR	Yes	Mobile	ELA	K–5	
cellulAR	bit.ly/3gByZ2V	AR	No	Mobile	Science	3–8	

Appendix AR/VR Resources

NAME	ACCESS	AR/VR	CREATION TOOL?	APP TYPE	SUBJECT	GRADE LEVEL	NEEDS
Class XR	apple.co/379Sqgg	AR & VR	Yes	Mobile and web	All	K–12, Higher Ed	iOS devices
CoSpaces	cospaces.io/edu	AR & VR	Yes	Mobile and web	All	K–12	
Curiscope Multiverse	bit.ly/3a2mzQo	AR	Yes	Mobile	Science	K–8	Posters for purchase
Devar	devar.org	AR & VR					
disruptED	disruptedx.com	AR & VR	No	Mobile	ELA	K–5	Books for purchase
DoodleLens	Google Play: bit.ly/37SbjmV iOS: apple.co/3oJpjX2	AR	Yes	Mobile	Art	K–5	

111

THE IMMERSIVE CLASSROOM

NAME	ACCESS	AR/VR	CREATION TOOL?	APP TYPE	SUBJECT	GRADE LEVEL	NEEDS
DottyAR	dottyar.com	AR	Yes	Mobile	All	K–12	QR code
DrawmaticAR	drawmaticar.com	AR	Yes	Mobile	ELA	K–5	Sheet
Engage	engagevr.io	VR	No	Web and VR app	All	6–12, Higher Ed	VR headset or install app on computer
eonXR	bit.ly/38eClFm	AR & VR	No	Mobile	All	6–12	
ERH Characters	experiencerealhistory.com	AR	No	Mobile	Social Studies	6–8	Optional cards, book, and board game
Expeditions	bit.ly/34nS1VG	AR & VR	No	Mobile	All	K–12	

Appendix AR/VR Resources

NAME	ACCESS	AR/VR	CREATION TOOL?	APP TYPE	SUBJECT	GRADE LEVEL	NEEDS
EyeJack	eyejackapp.com	AR	Yes	Mobile and web	All	K–12	
Face Replaced	apple.co/3gZDtR3	AR	Yes	Mobile	All	K–12	iOS only
Fectar	fectar.com	AR	Yes	Mobile	All	K–12	
Figment AR	viromedia.com/figment	AR	Yes	Mobile	All	K–12	
FlipgridAR	blog.flipgrid.com/news/ar	AR	Yes	Mobile and web	All	K–12	
Frame VR	framevr.io	VR	Yes	Mobile, web, and VR browser	All	K–12, Higher Ed	
Gadgeteer	gadgeteergame.com	VR	Yes	VR app	Science	6–12	VR headset

NAME	ACCESS	AR/VR	CREATION TOOL?	APP TYPE	SUBJECT	GRADE LEVEL	NEEDS
GeoGebra AR	geogebra.org/m/qbxbcmqw	AR	Yes	Mobile	Math	6–12	
Google AR	arvr.google.com/ar	AR	No	Mobile	All	K–12	
Google Earth	arvr.google.com/earth	VR	No	Mobile and web	All	K–12	
Google Translate	translate.google.com/?ui=tob	AR	Yes	Mobile and web	All	K–12	
Gravity Sketch	gravitysketch.com	VR	Yes	VR app	All	6–12, Higher Ed	VR headset
Halo AR	bit.ly/39Xhb0Q	AR	Yes	Mobile	All	K–12, Higher Ed	

Appendix AR/VR Resources

NAME	ACCESS	AR/VR	CREATION TOOL?	APP TYPE	SUBJECT	GRADE LEVEL	NEEDS
HoloGLOBE	bit.ly/2IGw7VY	AR	No	Mobile	Science	K–8	
Jig Workshop	jig.space/workshop.html	AR	Yes	Mobile	All	K–12	
JigSpace	jig.space	AR	No	Mobile App	STEM	K–12	
Kai's Clan	kaisclan.ai	AR & VR	Yes	Mobile and web	All	K–12	
LightSpace	logicalanimal.com/lightspaceapp	AR	Yes	Mobile	Art	K–12	
LightUp	lightup.io	AR	Yes	Mobile and web	All	K–12	

THE IMMERSIVE CLASSROOM

NAME	ACCESS	AR/VR	CREATION TOOL?	APP TYPE	SUBJECT	GRADE LEVEL	NEEDS
Lunch Rush	to.pbs.org/3gZW937	AR	No	Mobile	Math	K–5	Cards
NarratorAR	narratorar.com.au	AR	No	Mobile	ELA	K–1	
MagicPlan	magicplan.app	AR	Yes	Mobile	Math	6–12	
MEL Kids	melscience.com/US-en/kids/sets	AR	Yes	Mobile	Science	K–5	
MEL Science	melscience.com	VR	No	Mobile	Science	6–12	
MERGE Explorer	bit.ly/2LGVTua	AR & VR	No	Mobile	Science	K–8	MERGE cube
Metaverse	studio.gometa.io/landing	AR & VR	Yes	Mobile and web	All	K–12	

Appendix AR/VR Resources

NAME	ACCESS	AR/VR	CREATION TOOL?	APP TYPE	SUBJECT	GRADE LEVEL	NEEDS
MindLabs	exploremindlabs.com	AR	Yes	Mobile	Science	K–5	Cards and game pieces
Minecraft Earth	minecraft.net/en-us/about-earth	AR	Yes	Mobile	All	K–12	
Moatboat	moatboat.com	AR	Yes	Mobile	ELA	K–5	
Mootup	mootup.com	VR	Yes	Mobile, web, and VR browser			
Mozilla Hubs	hubs.mozilla.com	VR	Yes	Mobile, web, and VR browser	All	K–12, Higher Ed	
My Very Hungry Caterpillar AR	bit.ly/3h0cHrL	AR	No	Mobile	ELA	K–5	

NAME	ACCESS	AR/VR	CREATION TOOL?	APP TYPE	SUBJECT	GRADE LEVEL	NEEDS
mywebar.com	mywebar.com	AR	Yes	Web	All	K–12	
Nature Treks VR	naturetreksvr.com	VR	No	VR app	All	6–12	VR headset
Nearpod	nearpod.com	VR	Yes	Mobile and web	All	K–12	
Ocean Rift	bit.ly/2VZVOnq	VR	No	VR app	Science	6–12	VR headset
Object Viewer	bit.ly/33Vf5dR	AR	Yes	Mobile	All	K–12	
Photomath	photomath.app/en	AR	No	Mobile	Math	K–12	
Portals	apple.co/3mvoSy0	AR	Yes	Mobile	All	K–12	iOS devices only

Appendix AR/VR Resources

NAME	ACCESS	AR/VR	CREATION TOOL?	APP TYPE	SUBJECT	GRADE LEVEL	NEEDS
PuppetMaster	shmonster.com/puppetmaster	AR	Yes	Mobile	ELA	K–5	
Qlone	qlone.pro	AR	Yes	Mobile	All	K–12	
Quiver	quivervision.com	AR	Yes	Mobile	All	K–5	
Reality Composer	developer.apple.com/augmented-reality/tools	AR	Yes	Mobile	All	K–12	
RoomScan	locometric.com/roomscan	AR	Yes	Mobile	Math	6–12	
Rox's Secret Code	bit.ly/3qLQ27c	AR	Yes	Mobile	Tech	K–5	

119

NAME	ACCESS	AR/VR	CREATION TOOL?	APP TYPE	SUBJECT	GRADE LEVEL	NEEDS
RoundMe	roundme.com	VR	Yes	Mobile and web	All	K–12	
Scavengar	bit.ly/340LY9j	AR	Yes	Mobile	All	K–12	
SculptrVR	sculptrvr.com	VR	Yes	VR app	Art	3–12	VR headset
Sesgoritma	ardamavi.github.io/Sesgoritma-TheNewAge	AR	No	Mobile	All	K–12, Higher Ed	
SketchAR	sketchar.tech	AR	Yes	Mobile	Art	K–12	
Spoke	spokehub.co/ar	VR	Yes	Web	All	K–12: Higher Ed	

Appendix AR/VR Resources

NAME	ACCESS	AR/VR	CREATION TOOL?	APP TYPE	SUBJECT	GRADE LEVEL	NEEDS
Stickman AR	trulysocialgames.com/games/stickman-ar	AR	Yes	Mobile	LA & Art	K-5	
Storyfab	bit.ly/3gw7SpL	AR	Yes	Mobile	LA	K-5; 6-8	
StoryUp	story-up.com	VR	No	Mobile	LA	K-12	
Street View	google.com/streetview	VR	Yes	Mobile and web	All	K-12	
Supernatural	getsupernatural.com	VR	No	VR app	PE	Higher Ed	VR headset
Thyng	thyng.com	AR	Yes	Mobile	All	K-12	

THE IMMERSIVE CLASSROOM

NAME	ACCESS	AR/VR	CREATION TOOL?	APP TYPE	SUBJECT	GRADE LEVEL	NEEDS
Tilt Brush	tiltbrush.com	VR	Yes	VR app	All	6-12	VR headset
Tinkercad	tinkercad.com	AR	Yes	Web	All	K-12	
TokoToko	tokotoko.io	AR	Yes	Mobile	LA	3-8	
VictoryXR in Engage	victoryxr.com	VR	No	VR app	Science	6-12	VR headset
Virtual Speech	virtualspeech.com	VR	No	Mobile, web, and VR app	All	K-12	
Virtuali-tee	curiscope.com/products/virtuali-tee	AR	No	Mobile App	Science	K-5; 6-8	Tee shirt for purchase
Visible Body	visiblebody.com/ar	AR	No	Mobile	Science	9-12	

Appendix AR/VR Resources

NAME	ACCESS	AR/VR	CREATION TOOL?	APP TYPE	SUBJECT	GRADE LEVEL	NEEDS
WallaMe	walla.me	AR	Yes	Mobile	All	K–12	
Waypoint EDU	waypointedu.com	AR	Yes	Mobile	All	K–12	
WebXR	immersiveweb.dev	AR	Yes	Web	All	K–12	
WDR AR	bit.ly/2JOHv2w	AR	No	Mobile	Social Studies	6–12	
Wonderscope	wonderscope.com	AR	Yes	Mobile	LA	K–5	
World Brush	worldbrush.net	AR	Yes	Mobile	Art	K–12	
WWF Free-River	wwf.to/37Swcyn	AR	No	Mobile	Science	K–5	

THE IMMERSIVE CLASSROOM

NAME	ACCESS	AR/VR	CREATION TOOL?	APP TYPE	SUBJECT	GRADE LEVEL	NEEDS
YoPuppet	yopuppet.com	AR	Yes	Mobile	LA & Art	K–5	
YouTube	vr.youtube.com	VR	No	Mobile and web	All	K–12	
Zoe	zoe.com	VR	Yes	Web	All	6–12	VR headset

References

Abdelbary, M. (2017). Learning in Motion: Bring Movement Back to the Classroom. Education Week. Retrieved from http://bit.ly/3idZqwj

Berger, T. (2017). What We Lose With the Decline of Cursive. Edutopia. Retrieved from https://www.edutopia.org/article/what-we-lose-with-decline-cursive-tom-berger

Canadian Association of Optometrists. (n.d.). Are Virtual Reality Headsets Dangerous for Our Eyes? Retrieved from https://opto.ca/health-library/are-virtual-reality-headsets-dangerous-for-our-eyes

Centers for Disease Control and Prevention. (2020). Cleaning and Disinfection for Households. Retrieved from https://www.cdc.gov/coronavirus/2019-ncov/prevent-getting-sick/cleaning-disinfection.html

Gallagher, W. (2020). 'Apple Glass' may help users see better in low light using radar and LiDAR. Retrieved from http://bit.ly/38DceJz

Hollier, S. (2019). Augmented Reality and Accessibility. Retrieved from https://www.w3.org/WAI/APA/task-forces/research-questions/wiki/Augmented_Reality_and_Accessibility

Karsenti, T., Bugmann, J, and Gros, P. P. (2017) Transforming Education with Minecraft? Results of an exploratory study conducted with 118 elementary-school-students. Montréal : CRIFPE. Retrieved from https://bit.ly/2KAQCnt

Marr, B. (2019). What Is Extended Reality Technology? A Simple Explanation For Anyone. Forbes. Retrieved from http://bit.ly/2J04qaC

Microsoft Education. (2019). Immersive Reader is now available in MERGE Explorer. Microsoft Education Blog. Retrieved from https://bit.ly/3anLX36

Propeller Aerobotics Pty Ltd. (2020). Drone Photogrammetry: How Drone Photos Turn into 3D Surveys. Retrieved from https://www.propelleraero.com/blog/drone-photogrammetry-how-drone-photos-turn-into-3d-surveys/

Rahman, N. A., Mailok, R., & Husain, N. M. (2020). Mobile Augmented Reality Learning Application for Students with Learning Disabilities. International Journal of Academic Research in Business and Social Sciences, 10(2), 133–141.

Things Entertainment. (2017). Augmented Reality (AR) Accessibility Techniques - Part I. Retrieved from http://thingsentertainment.net/accessible_augmented_reality_techniques.html

The University of Melbourne. (1994 – 2017). Accessibility of Virtual Reality Environments. Retrieved from https://www.unimelb.edu.au/accessibility/guides/vr-old

Index

#
3D landscape scanning, 44
3D objects, 31-37, 38-41, 53, 60
3DoF, *see also* three degrees of freedom, 100
31DaysofARVRinEDU, 95-96
360-degree learning, 63-64
6DoF, *see also* six degrees of freedom, 45, 100

A
accessibility and AR/VR, 17, 18, 79
Adobe Aero, 33-34
Anima Res, 26, 75
Apple Watch, 73, 74
ARVRinEdu, Twitter handle, 4, 25, 26, 71, 95-96
ARVRinEdU blog, 95
AR creation, 31-34, 61-63
app hacking, 21-26
app smashing, 28-37
ARize, 4, 86, 94, 99
ARLOOPA, 4, 56, 58, 61, 97, 103
arthrogryposis, 19
artificial intelligence, 46
Assemblr, 4, 33, 62
AstroReality, 26
Atchison, Debra, 63
AugmentifyIt, 4, 26

B
Bambury, Steve, 91-92
BBC Civilisations, 110
breakouts, 54-55

C
Catchy Words AR, 12-14, 26,
challenge for students, 11
ClassImmerse, 26
ClassXR, 26
cleaning of devices, 49
coding, 69
CoSpaces, 4, 26, 33, 36, 54
COVID-19 pandemic, 49, 64, 79, 84, 103
creativity, tools to inspire, 24, 70
cross-platform learning, 46
Curiscope, 26, 76
Curran, Marialice, 79, 98

D
depression, treating, 84
device cleaning, 49
device management, 46
DisruptEd, 5, 69
dissection, virtual, 56, 59
DramaticAR, 68
Drezek, Michael, 84-86
dyslexia, 77

E
Edwards, Linda, 29-30
engagement, of reluctant students, 3
EON Reality, 26
escape rooms, 71-72
Explore Interactive, 26
EyeJack, 7, 19, 25, 27, 30, 34, 62
eye tracking, 46

F

FaceReplaced, 30
face filters, 66, 99
face shield, 79
Figment AR, 39
file types for 3D objects, 32
fitness trackers, 73
Flipgrid, 5, 29-30,
FrameVR, 39, 105

G

Global Maker Day, 106
Google Expeditions, 35, 63, 72
Google Poly, 23, 33
grants, 51
Gravity Sketch, 27, 39

H

Halo AR, 4, 12
hand tracking, 78, 100, 106
hearing impaired, 78-79
headsets, 48, 50, 56, 81
hidden messages, creating, 24

I

Immersive Learning Challenges, 3, 14, 19, 27, 41, 51, 64, 89, 107
immersive technology, benefits of 6-11
immersive technology, defined, 2
immersive technology, success stories, 12-14, 17-19, 77
immersive technology companies, 25-26
Insight Heart, 73
ISTE Standards for Educators, 100-102

J

Jig Workshop, *see also* JigSpace, 5, 60-61

K

Kai's Clan, 27, 40
kit ideas, 48-49
kit purchases, example, 50

L

Lake Shore Central Schools, 84
LIDAR, 44-45
LightUp, 4, 27
Limbix, 83
literacy apps, 66, 67, 78

M

Mansfield ISD, 49
medical procedures using AR/VR, 82-83
meeting spaces, VR, 38, 39, 47, 101-103
MERGE Cube, 29, 32, 33, 59
    make your own, 60
MERGE EDU, 29, 51
MERGE Explorer, 29, 30, 59-60, 80
Metaverse, 5, 26, 40, 71
Microsoft Immersive Reader, 80
Mindlabs, 72
mixed reality, 2
Moatboat, 26
Mozilla Hubs, 38, 103-104
Mr. Crumb's School for Disobedient Pets, 71-72
Murphree, Kim, 49
MyWebAR, 63

N

Narrator AR, 5, 26, 77
Nearpod, 26, 36, 39, 81
NuEyes, 81

O

Oculus, 26, 85
Oculus Quest, 39, 45, 71, 73

P

passion-based learning, 87
physical education, 73
Poth, Rachelle Dene, 22, 71
professional development, 89-93
PuppetMaster, 30
purchasing devices, 49

Q
Qlone, 26, 32-33, 37
QuantumERA, 26

R
reading apps, 67, 68
Reality Composer, 33
RemixVR, 39
reluctant readers, 80
remote learning, 43, 52, 61, 64, 83
robotics, 40
RoundMe, 36, 64
Rox's Secret Code, 69

S
Scavengar, 26, 33-34, 52-53
scavenger hunts, 53
science, 55-59
science labs, 55-59
selecting devices, 42, 44-46
Sesgoritma, 78
sign language, 78
six degrees of freedom (6DoF), 45, 100
social media, 92, 95
Spoke, 38, 104
standalone devices, 19, 45, 100
Stickman AR, 70
Storyfab, 34
storytelling apps, 34, 66-67
student need, identifying areas of, 16
Supernatural, 73
Street View, 23, 35-36, 39

T
Tilt Brush, 39, 84-85
three degrees of freedom (3DoF), 100
Tinkercad, 40
TokoToko, 70
Torch AR, 27
Tour Creator, 35-36, 63
Thyng, 27, 33

U
UtopiaVR, 104

V
Victory XR, 27
video tools, 30-31
Virtual Speech, 27
Virtuali-Tee, 75
visually impaired, 81

W
WallaMe app, 23-24
WebXR, 38, 47, 63, 104
wearable technology, 45, 73, 75
Whitaker, Tammy, 63
Wonderscope, 27, 68
writing, apps to inspire, 67-68

Y
YoPuppet, 31

Z
Zoe, 27, 37

If you enjoyed *The Immersive Classroom*, you may be interested in these similar ISTE titles.

Learning Transported: Augmented, Virtual and Mixed Reality for All Classrooms by Jaime Donally

This foundational guide to bringing immersive technology to the classroom features examples of AR, VR and MR; tips for selecting devices; lesson plans and ideas for using readily available AR/VR tools in the classroom.

Learn more or order at iste.org/TransportLearning

Immerse Yourself: Create Engaging AR/VR Experiences for All Learners

Based on the book *Learning Transported* by Jaime Donally, this laminated reference guide provides practical insights and examples to help any classroom teacher incorporate immersive tech into curriculum.

Learn more or order at iste.org/ImmersJSG

Chart A New Course: A Guide to Teaching Essential Skills for Tomorrow's World by Rachelle Dene Poth

This book shows educators how to help students develop essential skills through authentic, real-world learning experiences, building a pathway for the future of learning and work.

Learn more or order at iste.org/EssentialSkills

Learn as a team with ISTE books!

ISTE's bulk books program makes team-based PD a breeze, and you'll save 35% or more off the retail price when you order large quantities. Email books@iste.org for details. ISTE members get 25% off every day!

Shop all print and ebook titles at iste.org/books

Augmented and Virtual Reality for All Learners

Learning from 2D to 3D

Spending an enormous amount of time researching the best AR/VR tools is not only impractical but unnecessary.

Build the foundation for successful augmented and virtual reality implementation with in-depth training and practical classroom application.

Topics include:
- Getting started with AR/VR
- AR/VR for young learners
- Creating a virtual classroom
- Immersive scavenger hunts
- Building virtual tours
- AR/VR creation

Jaime Donally is an author, speaker, and founder of the ARVRinEDU and Global Maker Day communities.

Practical Use of Immersive Technology
Easy, Innovative, Transformative

www.arvrinedu.com

www.ingramcontent.com/pod-product-compliance
Lightning Source LLC
Chambersburg PA
CBHW081453070526
44586CB00019B/2334